What Is Your
ROADBLOCK
To Fulfillment?

*A guide to continue the growth you started
in the 8 areas of life*

Samuel P. "Pat" Black III

Flourish Summit Publishing
Erie, Pennsylvania

First Edition, July 2013

Flourish Summit Publishing
121 East 2nd Street
Erie, PA 16507

Published in the United States by Flourish Summit Publishing, a division of Black Interest Limited Partnership, Erie, Pennsylvania.

ISBN: 978-0-9894575-3-8

Printed in the United States of America

Contents

Foreword

I met Pat Black in 2002 and immediately recognized him as a student who is extremely bright and incredibly motivated to not only apply his learnings to his own life, but also to make a difference in the world by bringing these learnings to others. Pat studied many different spiritual practices and with various personal growth trainers. With me, Pat studied Huna and Neuro-Linguistic Programming (NLP), both of which are featured in this book.

This book demonstrates several points that I think are critical:

True personal/spiritual growth is not achieved through *theory* but through *practice*. I've seen too many students become workshop junkies, attending workshop after workshop, weekend after weekend always seeking the latest guru de jour. They feel unsatisfied and can't figure out why, since they *know* so much, they still feel unfulfilled. Their latest workshop high only lasts until Tuesday or Wednesday because they haven't realized that the real learning comes from applying that weekend wisdom to everyday life, Monday through Friday as well as weekends, morning 'til night.

Being holy on Sundays then hating your coworkers starting Monday morning is not the path to unconditional love. Finding deep peace by spending one day in silent retreat means nothing if you let road rage take over in the first traffic jam you hit. A shift in consciousness does not happen by dipping your toes in the water, talking eloquently about it, then going on your merry way to live your life as you've always lived it. As Pat points out, it's important to *live* what you learn and apply your practice to *all* areas of your life.

The basics are the foundation of any personal or spiritual growth. There are certain universal basics that most spiritual paths acknowledge, though each tradition uses different terminology. In this book, Pat lays these basics out using terminology of Huna and NLP: perception is projection, cause and effect, creation and dichotomies, cycles and rhythms, functions of conscious and unconscious minds, ecology, and flexibility. If you don't know about or refuse to accept these basics, you'll find yourself in a losing battle. It's like gravity: You may not fully understand why gravity works or even like that it works the way it does. But gravity doesn't really care what you think. It will work *exactly* as it's supposed to work every time you leap off a tall building (which may turn out to be just once!).

That's how the universal basics operate: reliably, impersonally, without exception. The point is not to "evolve beyond" these basics but to learn to work with them and recognize them in action.

Our relationship to the unconscious mind is critical to the expansion of consciousness. I recently published an entire book on the unconscious mind. It is the direct connection between the conscious mind and Higher Self. It isn't a "lesser mind" and shouldn't be dismissed as merely the "animal instinct" side of ourselves. It is often where our greatest passion, capacity, wisdom, and energy is housed.

In Western culture, the unconscious mind has been given a bum rap. And though in recent years, we've figured out that the unconscious mind is a powerhouse, Westerners still treat the unconscious as subservient to the conscious mind, trying to bludgeon it into submission via affirmations. As Pat points out throughout this book, that simply doesn't work. The unconscious mind has a wisdom and a knowing that we need to listen to and honor.

We need to pay attention to the dark. Often times, the very lessons that are most important for our growth come in the form of pain: failure in business, dysfunction in relationship, fear of being who we really are. As someone once said, "It's a gift that comes in horrible wrapping!" It is a gift, and the "horrible wrapping" is simply a way of getting our attention and nudging us toward growth. As Pat points out, we can use those gifts by looking into them, acknowledging our responsibility, and looking for the learnings behind them. The strategies we have always used to deal with these dark gifts may not be the strategies that serve us now.

The dark also includes the Shadow, that part of our unconscious mind that we think we are not – or wish we were not! But the Shadow is not a mistake, it's also a gift. Accepting the Shadow allows us to unleash our inherent creativity and passion to live fuller, more empowered lives.

As you read this book, I invite you to apply the learnings to yourself, give time to the exercises Pat offers, and incorporate what you learn to all areas of your own life. In that way, you will experience it's true value.

Mahalo,

Dr. Matt James

International trainer, author, and President of The Empowerment Partnership

Introduction

Over 3,000 years ago, Egypt was known as a beacon of light throughout the world. A powerful civilization, leaders from foreign nations courted the pharaohs to avoid military take-over and sought the rich produce of the nation to avoid famine in their own lands. But beyond being a military, trade, and agricultural power, Egypt was known to distant seekers of the "sacred sciences" for its mystery schools and the magi, priests, and priestesses who taught within them. Pythagoras is said to have studied there, as well as Jesus of Nazareth.

Not a lot is known about the daily routines and intricacies of the mystery schools that were built along the Nile. But it is believed that the Egyptian mystery schools taught qualified initiates to achieve full consciousness, psychic abilities, and even immortality by learning to control the mind and body. According to ancient teachings, the temples themselves were constructed using sophisticated geometrical patterns, proportions and symbols designed to provoke insights and represent specific lessons. Some even believe that the field created by each temple's design could literally alter and heal a student's physical, mental, and spiritual bodies, expanding the student's capacity to understand and learn.

Students who became initiates of these mystery schools were clear that the training would be rigorous for body, soul, and spirit. Their faculties of will, intuition, and reason had to be developed to an exceptional level, which meant a total restructuring of the student's physical, moral, and spiritual being. Only then could they gain access to the secrets and forces of the universe and become masters themselves.

Training in the mystery school is said to have been structured in a series of initiations. They started at the "Outer Door," then moved inward through additional doors as they mastered each lesson. If a lesson could not be mastered, the initiate could not move forward and the next door would not be revealed to them.

One of the most important aspects of the mystery schools was the breaking down of everything the seeker knew or thought he knew. The student literally had to face death – and some actually died – in order to release all the spiritual potential within. Only those who were willing to face physical and psychological death became fully empowered and initiated into all of the mysteries.

The mystery schools were designed to take a sacred science seeker through an intense, experiential curriculum with the goal of total mastery. In a sense, my plans for creating the Flourishing Centers are built on this concept. Though students at the centers are not brought to the brink of "death" as in the ancient tradition, we know it's critical that we be willing to give up old patterns, comfort zones, and ways of coping in order to become open to true empowerment. So part of the process has to be identifying and releasing those patterns which may have served us at one

point in our lives, but now have become roadblocks to our

growth.

About Me

I was raised in Pennsylvania in a fairly conservative and prominent family. My father's mother was an Evangelical Presbyterian and my mother was Catholic. They all believed that children should learn to fear their parents as the ultimate authorities and their child rearing reflected that belief. To survive, I learned to be passive/aggressive, to acquiesce on the surface while rebelling when I was out of my parents' sight.

I was sent to a traditional Catholic grade school, complete with nuns in scary habits wielding vicious rulers. I realized early on that I was "different" from other kids in the way I thought. Rather than towing the line, I was determined to uncover what was exciting, forbidden, and hidden beneath the nuns' teachings. Clearly, that did not make me a popular student, and I felt frustrated that no one would explain why we were supposed to learn what was being taught.

I went to a public high school and became involved in sports. I had a couple of teachers who acted as mentors to me, but I still felt "different" and out of my element. That feeling lasted through college at Penn State and during my years in the military in the mid '60's after college.

When I got out of the military, I followed the old maxim of "take the first good paying job that you're offered" and I accepted a position with a large insurance company. Though I did pretty well there, I became disenchanted with the way the company was run. It was clear that to get promoted you had to play the game, which meant sucking up to whoever had the power to promote you. I saw too many brilliant people get over-looked, while those who were more incompetent – but better at "playing the game" – got ahead. After several years, I left to go home and work at my dad's insurance agency.

I didn't become interested in personal growth or the esoteric until around 1995. I had entered therapy because, although I was to all outward appearances a success, I felt an almost constant sense of rage along with a sense that something critical was missing from my life. Through the therapeutic experience, I was able to recognize and release a lot of the patterns and roadblocks that had been stifling and enraging me. Once those obstacles were gone, my life expanded dramatically! I was able to initiate a dozen different enterprises, all of which seemed to fall into place easily and organically.

I found myself becoming more of a social entrepreneur, involving myself in ventures that make a specific, positive contribution to the world in which we live. I founded Erie Management Group, LLC to invest, create, and manage companies with innovative products to capitalize on economic opportunities in the Lake Erie Region. Through that group, we created HERO Bx, LLC, one of the largest biodiesel manufacturers in the Northeast. I also founded the Blackstone Ranch Institute in Taos, New Mexico, which provides targeted seed money for innovative efforts in environmental sustainability, sustainable business practices, renewable energies, and green employment. My wife Susan and I purchased 191 acres of an old ranch in the Taos Valley to develop and demonstrate the best environmental practices for sustainable ranching and farming utilizing modern solar, wind, and geothermal technologies.

Along with my business ventures, I co-founded The Black Family Foundation, which is an active grant-maker, partner in philanthropy, and leader in helping build vital and sustainable non-profit enterprises. Since 1994, the Foundation has promoted innovation in education, health care, workforce development, and the arts in the Erie region. Our philanthropic ventures have spread knowledge, innovation, and environmentally sustainable practices throughout the United States. Through all of this work, I continue to make a contribution that I feel is uniquely mine.

Removing my roadblocks and negative patterns not only opened up my business life but also my spiritual life. At an early age, I had rejected the religions of my family. With this new personal awareness, I became interested in the esoteric, shamanism, Huna, and Buddhism, as well as in-depth personal growth from the psychological perspective, such as Neuro-Linguistic Programming.

As I studied these varied disciplines and walked these diverse spiritual paths, I realized a couple of things. First, I realized that the key to my accepting real change and growth had come from my willingness to recognize and release the roadblocks and negative patterns that were running my life. I realized that this is not just the path I had to take - that all of us must "die" to who we were to become who we are meant to be – just like the ancient mystery schools taught. And once that dying or release has happened, the opening to spiritual realms is automatic.

Next, it occurred to me that one size does not fit all. In a room of 300 people listening to the guru de jour, there are 300 individuals with 300 different personalities, backgrounds, life experiences, and understandings. As wise as the teacher at the front of the room might be, these large group settings cannot offer the direct insight and teaching that each person needs to take him or her to the next level.

It also became apparent that a spiritual path is an ongoing process. A weekend workshop or a month long retreat is not enough to get us to what most of us are seeking, whether you call it enlightenment or empowerment or self-actualization or mastery. We need ongoing support and ongoing learning. But most of us are also not in position (nor do we have the inclination) to give up our lives and our livelihoods to sit at the feet of a master or on the blanket of a shaman. Most churches are not geared toward teaching personal enlightenment and even if they were, a few hours on the pews one day per week doesn't cut it either.

Another point that became clear to me was that the path to get where we wanted to be spiritually had to be experiential and applied to everyday life. It isn't just about knowledge and concept and theory. Being able to spout spiritual homilies or discuss universal principles is simply the booby prize. What we are really seeking is the living, breathing expression of the "What Is" through our own lives. Like the mystery schools, to get where we want to go requires experiential teaching that alters us in mind, emotion, body, and spirit.

So I began to wonder: How could that kind of individualized support, teaching, and experiential training be made available? This question was the seed of the Flourishing Centers.

The Flourishing Centers

The Flourishing Centers will be intentionally located in places on the planet where the energy is right for a particular chakra and its learning. For example, the Flourishing Center for the first chakra will be in Taos, New Mexico because the energy is so strong there that it draws people's issues up to the surface. Once these issues surface, the learning is to deal with them and come to resolution. The third chakra's center will be located in Erie, Pennsylvania because the energy in that area is all about developing strong will. If you don't have a strong will in Erie, you'll likely get run over! The center for the learnings of the fourth chakra will be located in Kona, Hawaii because the energy there is so heart based. Other centers will be similarly located.

The Centers will be built when the timing is right, when a sufficient number of people are ready to do this intensive personal work so that each center is worthwhile and sustainable.

Many of us have experienced various group processes for personal growth, which is fine for learning the basics. However, each of us is different and unique so one size does not fit all. The Flourishing Centers will offer an individual mentoring process for those who desire to go deeper than the basics. How long each individual will stay in each center will depend on his or her desire for growth and how long he or she needs to go through the process.

This Book

This book will take you through some of the curriculum that will be taught at the Flourishing Centers. First, you'll find an overview of some basic spiritual principles that span most paths of expanded consciousness. In that overview, I especially draw from two disciplines: Huna, the indigenous spiritual path of the Hawaiian Islands, and Neuro-Linguistic Programming (NLP), a set of psychotherapeutic techniques that work with the unconscious and conscious minds. But these same principles are found in many other paths. Even if you think you are familiar with these principles, I ask that you not skip over that chapter! I'll be using that terminology throughout this book and I want us to have the same understanding of the concepts. Also, frankly, many of us who have been on the path for a while have become jaded. We learned the principles long ago but have become lax in applying them. A little review definitely can't hurt! And a misunderstanding or misuse of the basics can definitely be a roadblock to your fulfillment. After the basics, I'll discuss your personal survival

mechanism, what it is, how to identify it, and how to release it.

We'll talk about how the basics and your survival mechanism

affect all eight areas of your life: relationships, career, health &

fitness, spirituality, personal growth & development, inner

technology, history, and family. Again, even if you think you've

got a certain area of life nailed, that you have become a master in

a certain aspect of your life so don't need to look into it further,

please don't skip that chapter! I heard a golf instructor once say

that whatever foible you have in your golf swing, that foible will

show up in every stroke from your putt to your drive off the tee.

So if you have a particular weakness or misunderstanding in one

area of your life, odds are good that this same misunderstanding

is in other areas. It may be more subtle. It may be masked. But it's

likely still there. So use every area as rich ground for self-

investigation.

For each area, I've offered specific practices so you can discover your roadblocks and release them experientially. These practices or exercises are meant to fit into your busy life, not to be set aside until you have extra time. When do we ever really get that extra time anyway? And hopefully, you will find yourself incorporating these practices into your life going forward.

Chapter 1: The Basics

I overheard someone complaining about having to take a lengthy spiritual path. "Why does it have to be so hard? Why can't I just get enlightened like Eckhart Tolle? Just sit on a park bench for a couple years then – ZAM! – get hit with enlightenment."

Most of us are not hit with enlightenment like some lightning bolt from a Universal Intelligence. Most of us have to schlump along, lesson by lesson, until we have enough lessons under our belts that it starts coming together. At the times when our schlumping seems all uphill, that lightning bolt, though kind of scary, sounds pretty attractive.

But the problem with the lightning bolt of enlightenment is that it often doesn't last because the basics underlying that enlightenment aren't fully grasped. It's like having an incredible natural singing talent. That talent can get you pretty far. But without the knowledge of how to use your instrument properly, you're likely to burn it out and limit what you can do with it. Lightning bolt enlightenment can be ungrounded, elusive, and insubstantial when it comes to living life through its lens.

Another problem with instant enlightenment is that it's hard to express and even harder to explain. Think about the things at which you are an expert. You can probably teach someone those areas of expertise that you learned step by step. But what about those areas of innate genius? The capabilities you were just born with and that seem so inherent to you? Aren't those more difficult to teach or even put into words? For example, in my life I've had an innate ability to create new companies. I also have the ability to see the entire big picture, to be a visionary. Having a vision and having the ability to transform that vision into a reality are two different talents; many people have one or the other, but not both. Envisioning a project is very natural and easy for me.

18

Explaining that vision to someone who thinks very differently than I do isn't simple at all. I've learned through the years that it takes time to get others to understand the vision so they are on board and in alignment with it and the end results I envision. Because being a visionary comes so easily to me, I can't say that I've been able to teach someone who is not naturally a visionary to become one. But because putting together a company is a step-by-step process, I've been able to teach others how to do that.

So schlumping along the path, taking it step by step, turns out to be more reliable and highly beneficial. The learning runs deep, especially during those uphill climbs. Along this route, here are some of the basics you need to know:

Perception is Projection

The principle of "perception is projection" basically says that you create your reality. It's not that you create the desk across the room or the stars in the sky. It means that everything you take in through your senses is filtered in a certain way that is based on your individual DNA, your history, the decisions you have made along the way. And within this filtering system, you actually decide what you will see and what you will remain blind to. It's as if you have a huge IMAX screen in front of you. Instead of a film projector in the background, you are the one creating all the images on it. What you love and what you hate internally will all show up on that screen externally. Let me give some examples.

I heard about a couple who sponsored a young student in Africa. They hadn't heard from him for a while but then received an email saying that he had decided to do some extra course work during the vacation months. He was requesting additional

20

financial support from them to cover the expenses. The wife's

instant reaction was, "Really? After not communicating for so

long, he just writes when he wants more money?" In contrast, her

husband's reaction was, "Isn't that great! He's doing extra work

and he trusts us enough to ask for support!" The situation was

exactly the same, right? But the reality that the wife created was

entirely different than that of her husband.

By the way, in this case, the wife decided that her husband's

perspective was much better so she decided to adopt it. This

brings up another important point: we are clear that our

perceptions are not Real with a capital R, but are only projections.

We realize that we have some choice in how we perceive things.

Say for instance you have an uncle who used to tease you

unmercifully when you were a kid. As you go through life, you

encounter people who unconsciously remind you of that uncle.

Odds are that you dislike them on sight, that you don't trust them though you can't explain why, that you feel defensive around them. These people who physically or energetically remind you of that uncle may be totally innocent. But your filters tell you otherwise. Your choice point is to step back and think about your reaction. Does how you feel about the person in front of you *really* match their actions? Would perceiving them differently serve you better? Is there some lesson here?

The thing about perception is projection is that the things we perceive, especially the things that make us uncomfortable, have some message or learning for us— but only if we remember that this is what's going on. For example, one hectic day I was driving on the highway, late for an appointment, when a little old lady pulled right in front of me and slowed down to about 30 miles per hour – grrrr! After I'd gnashed my teeth for a while, I took a deep breath and remembered that I had a choice. So I asked myself the question: If this little old lady is here to teach me something, what might it be? And I realized that I'd been running too hard for a while and needed to slow down.

Same situation but two totally different perceptions of it, two different "realities." One was that the little old lady was a frustrating obstacle that threatened to ruin my morning. The other was that she came as a gift, a reminder to take care of myself. Interestingly enough, as soon as I perceived her as a gift, she took the next exit and got out of my way.

The main points to grasp about the principle of "perception is projection" are: a) everything you perceive is based on your internal "realities" and not some ultimate truth, b) if you stay aware of that fact, you will realize that you have choice about how you perceive things, c) often people and situations show up with a learning or message if we pay attention, and d) if we catch the lesson, our internal "realities" can shift.

23

Cause and Effect

This principle is, on the surface, pretty straightforward. What you do causes a particular something to happen. You flick on a light switch, a light bulb comes on. You neglect to pay a bill and the bill collector calls. You run head first into a brick wall and you'll give yourself a tremendous headache!

The important point of cause and effect along the path to empowerment is to live our lives on the cause side of the coin, not the effect. Living from the effect side is the classic victim syndrome of "life is doing it to me." It's seeing ourselves as a victim to the circumstances and movement around us. From this place, we have no power, no choice, no ability to do much of anything except get smashed against the rocks in a river. The victim claims that "she made me angry" or "the economy ruined me financially."

Being "at cause" is to acknowledge that we create our own reality. If in some form I "caused" the little old lady to pull in front of me and slow down, it's clearer that I am then responsible for how I decide to respond to it. Being on the cause side allows us to be powerful, to choose, to create our own options of how we respond. It's a place of total responsibility for the outcomes of our own lives.

One tricky thing about cause and effect is that the effect can happen at the same time as the cause or even precede the cause! Though we live in a time-bound material world that moves in linear fashion, the universe itself does not. Time and space are illusions. As Albert Einstein pointed out, "The only reason for time is so that everything doesn't happen at once." He also said that "The distinction between the past, present, and future is only a persistently stubborn illusion." Problem is that many of us take this illusion too seriously and it thwarts our efforts at growth.

For example, a student of mine was somewhat addicted to time. She wanted everything to unfold faster than it naturally did. She would find herself frustrated as she tried to control the process and speed up her learning. The lesson for her was to let go and let the process unfold in its own illusionary timeframe. Personal/spiritual growth has no set schedule. Once she got that concept, she found the freedom to walk through life with more peace and equanimity.

Creation and Dichotomies

The principle of creation and dichotomies is basically like Sir Isaac Newton's third law of motion: Every action has an equal and opposite reaction. Most spiritual teachers would say that whenever we create, think, or feel, the opposite creation, thought, or feeling comes into being at the same instant. The universe is constantly balancing itself with night and day, light and dark, hot and cold, up and down. But it's like a teeter-totter with two kids on it: it's rarely stopped at the perfect balance point but always in motion. This constant balancing motion is reflected in us as well. So how does it work?

On the mental/emotional side, psychologists talk about the Shadow of our unconscious minds. The Shadow houses all of the thoughts and feelings we reject because those "opposite" thoughts and feelings have to be somewhere. For instance, a woman who rejects the emotion of anger will have a molten volcano full of anger deep inside her Shadow self, just waiting to explode. The man who rejects his softer, more feminine side will hide a vulnerable, soft self within. The stronger the position that we hold consciously, the stronger the opposite position is in the Shadow.

Our opposites also show up in the exterior world as reflective mirrors. Take for example the person who considers herself highly responsible. Suddenly, all she sees around her are others who are seemingly irresponsible and she becomes irritated. "What's the matter with them? Don't they know they have to be accountable for their lives?" Remember that perception is projection. Her perception of others and her reaction are clear indications that opposites are at play – and these opposites want to be accepted. The moment she acknowledges that part of herself that is not taking responsibility in life is the moment that all of those "irresponsible" people disappear or suddenly become accountable!

Cycles and Rhythms

Everything in the universe operates in cycles and rhythms caused by the energy exchange between the dichotomies, that constant movement of balance and imbalance. Everything in your own system – your physical body, emotional life, mental activity, spiritual self – also operates within cycles and rhythms. The trick is that these four parts of you each have their own natural cycles and rhythms that are set at different speeds. So these parts of yourself are rarely in synch.

There's a hierarchy to these four parts of yourself. The most powerful, yet the most simple is the spiritual self. Right below the spiritual self is the mental level, which is quite powerful as well and which controls our perceptions and projections. The emotional level is comprised of emotions that are driven by chemicals released in the brain. In addition, we experience feelings which are comprised of the combination of emotions plus thoughts. On the path to growth, we can allow our emotions and our feelings to run us or we can control them to our advantage. The physical body, more complex than the other levels, is actually the least powerful level of ourselves.

Historically, western culture has gotten the power structure backwards. We look at an Arnold Schwarzenegger type as powerful simply because of his brawn and muscle. But martial arts show that through emotional control, mental concentration, and spiritual connection, the 90-pound "weakling" can easily overpower the Incredible Hulk!

Our job with the cycles and rhythms is not necessarily to change them. It's to track them, to be aware of where we are physically, emotionally, mentally, and spiritually. Personal/spiritual growth is not a linear process but one that is cyclical. Along the path, we have our various learnings, which include "speed bumps" that pop up the minute we decide to change or grow.

It's like remodeling your home. You may have lived in it for years with no seeming maintenance issues or problems. But the moment you take a sledgehammer to knock down a wall, you find all sorts of things, not related to the actual remodeling project, that need to be repaired. Before you can achieve your desired result, you have to fix those little problems that you didn't even know existed.

When we make the decision to change and grow, we have put out the energy that we are ready to accept the challenge. Many of the lessons we experience along the way may not seem to have anything to do with what we are working toward – but this is how the energy of change works. It's like peeling away the layers of an onion. On the journey, at times it will seem as if the same learning you already experienced pops up again. But you're really hitting a similar place on the cycle at a deeper level. In the natural flow of energy, you learn a piece of what you need to learn then the energy calms down until it is time to learn the next piece.

Conscious/Unconscious

Of course, there have been volumes written about the conscious and unconscious mind. For our purposes here, it's just important to know their functions. The conscious mind's only function is to choose "yes" or "no." It chooses to focus on something or ignore it. It chooses to go after a goal or not go for it. It chooses to move toward self-discovery or abandon it.

The unconscious is like a huge complex of underground caverns. It is completely dark, ranging for miles in any direction. When we bring our conscious mind to it to discover what is hidden inside, it's as if we carry a small penlight. Our penlight only illuminates the tiniest bit of the cavern while all the rest remains in darkness. But to make the discoveries that we need to make, we need to take that penlight and illuminate what we can.

Ecology

The principle of ecology says that the decisions you make about who you are in the world affect everything around you – which in turn affect you. So the question should be asked, "How will this impact me, my family, my community, my nation, my planet?" If something feels good for you alone but not the rest of the ecological system, something is off and needs to be investigated.

A choice you make may upset someone in your sphere – but is it

really harming him or her? The best decisions have some positive

(or at least neutral) impact on your entire world.

Another part of ecology is that how you behave in the world is

how the world will treat you. If you run your life with integrity,

transparency, and authenticity, odds are that you will be

surrounded by people who treat you in the same manner. On the

other hand, if you experience life as a dog eat dog struggle for

survival, you'll probably experience a lot of snarling and scratching

and biting in everything from your marriage to your career.

Flexibility

The principle of flexibility asks, "How flexible is your response to

life's situations and circumstances?" As babies, we have incredible

flexibility. We can sit in a restaurant and, if our needs aren't being met, we can easily scream our heads off! But as adults, we often become rigid and confined in our responses. How many of us wouldn't even send a bad dish back in a restaurant or leave a conversation that had turned nasty before the meal is done? Our social conventions have limited our flexibility in response.

But worse than social convention, it is our personal survival strategies (which we discuss in the next chapter) that force us to react in a particular way. You know the feeling: Someone hits our "hot button" and we feel like we have no choice but to explode or feel wounded or get defensive. Some small voice may be saying, "But I don't want to react this way! I'm not really like this!" But our physiology takes over and that visceral reaction has its way with us.

The principle of flexibility says that we have the ability to respond, not just react. Response feels balanced, takes the ecology of the situation into consideration, feels fluid with various options.

Reaction, on the other hand, feels like a frantic imperative to defend oneself at any cost!

Psychologists are throwing the word "plasticity" around a lot these days. Psychological researchers have discovered that the brain is not frozen as was previously thought, but can be changed, rewired neuron by neuron. So though we may have certain reactions (personal survival strategies) wired into our brains, we do have the ability to be rewired and enhance our flexibility of choices.

What To Do with the Basics

So that is a brief overview of some basic concepts. In the next chapter, we'll talk about one of the biggest roadblocks to your growth and fulfillment: that personal survival strategy that you developed as a child. However, the basics in this chapter can become roadblocks as well, if they are misused or misunderstood. Let me give a couple of examples:

I met a woman in a group therapy session I was helping to run. "Mary" was in her seventies and had joined the group to help her deal with her cancer, which was terminal. After a few sessions, it became very clear Mary refused to accept any darkness in her life. She was traditionally religious and determined to remain pure and saintly. The problem was that this didn't allow the "dark" side – that side of her that wanted to scream and swear and curse God for her condition – to be expressed. She would not allow this darkness its powerful expression, so it suffocated her. Mary's big roadblock was in misunderstanding the principle of creation and dichotomies. Rather than understanding that we are all made up of light and dark, Mary feared that she would become the dark if she allowed its expression. By clinging to the light and rejecting the dark, she found herself completely stuck.

Another example would be the person who misunderstands the law of cause and effect. This person goes through life thinking that he is on the "effect" side of the equation. He is the victim of whatever life tosses him. In a sense, it can be comforting because he gets to blame circumstances and others for his sorry state. But this stance blocks him from moving forward and leaves him trapped and powerless to change his condition.

So it's important to note that the basics will support you in your continued growth if you understand them and apply them correctly. But used incorrectly, they will sabotage and prevent your fulfillment.

Chapter 2: Your Personal Survival Strategy

Misunderstanding or misusing one of the basics can be a roadblock to your continued growth. But I think the most powerful roadblock can be your personal survival strategy. This strategy remains unconscious until you unearth it, but it pretty much runs your entire life. Your strategy is developed in childhood, often in reaction to a particular situation or person. But as time goes on, this survival strategy becomes generalized to just about all situations and people who might be potentially harmful in any way. Sometimes the repercussions of this type of roadblock becomes so overwhelming that we self-medicate (alcohol and legal or illegal drugs) to get away from them – all the while not really seeing what part the roadblock has played.

There is an ancient saying that basically declares: *If you bring forth what is in you, you will save yourself. If you don't bring forth what is in you, you will kill yourself.* An important part of "what is in you" is your personal survival strategy, and that strategy is housed in the unconscious. The good news is that we don't necessarily have to search out our survival strategy by taking our penlight into the cavern of the unconscious. We get a lot of clues about this strategy through patterns that show up in the eight areas of life, as we will discuss in later chapters. These eight areas of life are actually our access points to uncovering our roadblocks.

Creating Our Strategy

As children, we are thrust into a world with all kinds of real and imagined dangers. We're too small and too naïve to deal with these threats directly but our little amygdalae are pumped up to help us survive. Though we have limited knowledge of how the world operates and how best to protect ourselves, we are still survival-oriented enough to come up with a strategy to help keep us "safe." These strategies are developed and firmly in place by the time we're six or seven years old. By the time we are adults, our personal survival strategies have become deeply rooted in the unconscious mind. Though we may have a few survival strategies, usually most of us choose one core strategy as our default. Whenever we perceive a threat —BAM! — that childhood strategy leaps up and takes charge often without our even noticing.

So let me ask you: If you as an adult were facing a difficult situation or some type of danger, would you really seek out a seven year old for guidance on how to handle it? Unless that seven year old is the Dalai Lama, probably not. But in a sense, this is what is happening when your personal survival strategy takes over. This strategy was formed and created by a very young child and, though they may have done the trick during childhood, usually those strategies are not very useful as an adult. But, because your personal survival is so deeply ingrained in the neurology of your brain, it remains powerful and is usually your first and strongest reaction in times of stress.

My parents firmly believed in the "spare the rod, spoil the child" theory of childrearing. Whenever I crossed the line or crossed my father, he felt it his duty to grab the broom and beat the tar out of me! Clearly, I needed a survival strategy to avoid the beatings.

The one I chose was the passive/aggressive strategy (which is a common choice for children in verbally or physically abusive situations). I came to understand that when I agreed with my parents – "Yes, sir!" "Yes, ma'am!" – I was safe. No broom. So I made sure to appear to agree, to acquiesce, to obey. But the rebellious, independent side of me couldn't quite leave it at that. So though I appeared to agree with my parents' demands and wishes, behind their backs I did whatever I damn well pleased!

As a young child, this was an okay strategy. I got to do what I wanted yet didn't inspire the wrath of my father. But take this same strategy into adult relationships and you can see how dysfunctional it could get. My passive/aggressive strategy popped

42

up with every authority figure: "You think you're such a big shot? Sure, I'll pretend to go along with you but then watch me take you down a peg or two!" It was there within my marriage: "You don't want me to do that? Fine, I won't – at least not until you're not looking!" When I would actually acquiesce to others' desires, for example when I accepted the first job offered to me when I got out of the military, it wouldn't take long for the aggressive side of the coin to rear its head and become an almost unmanageable rage!

I even had some vague sense that my personal survival strategy (though I didn't recognize it as such) was not working for me. But it was so ingrained into my neurology that I honestly didn't see my reactions as optional. I would encounter a perceived threat and my entire system would instantly power up into passive/aggressive mode. Much of the time, I wasn't even aware that I was doing it. But like most of us, when I was aware of what I was doing, I convinced myself that my reactions were justified.

The "addiction" I used to self-medicate from the pain of this strategy was to stay planted in the analytical mind, which allowed me to numb out all emotion.

Other Strategies

The passive/aggressive strategy is common. But there are others. For example, being purely passive is a strategy. It's like the clever strategy of the opossum playing dead. An opossum has an involuntary comatose-like state that is induced by extreme fear. Some predators are stimulated to eat by the chase and the kill. These predators are less attracted to an inert opossum because the predator's appetite has not been excited. They will leave the opossum alone. As a child, this little one would seek to be "seen and not heard." As an adult, a person with this strategy would never voice an opinion, never disagree or question, and in many ways seek to be invisible in life.

Some children choose the purely aggressive strategy. They become like little badgers who are aggressive when cornered, even if their aggressor is much bigger than they are. Often these children will displace the aggression and, rather than attack their attackers, take their anger and frustration out on smaller kids or animals. They become the bullies of the playground. As adults, their mottos might be "The best defense is a good offense." They may pick unnecessary fights or arguments and be perceived as contentious.

Other children remove themselves from the difficulties of life by living in fantasy worlds. These "head in the clouds" types often grow up relating more to their fictional world than real life. On the positive side, they may become artists or writers. On the negative side, they can become totally disconnected from the necessities of day-to-day life.

Others become rigid, needing to control their environments in whatever ways possible. Unable to control the reactions of their parents or the world around them, they become obsessed with controlling every tiny detail they can control. If things are not done "just so," these children become anxious. Children with this survival strategy often become perfectionists as adults. The extreme of this is the psychopath or sociopath that fears he will die if he does not follow his urges, the imperatives of his controlling nature, no matter how bizarre.

You may recognize your childhood survival strategy in the examples above or yours may be slightly different. The point to grasp is that we all, without exception, developed a survival strategy to cope with life as children. And the vast majority of us have carried that strategy forward as adults. Perhaps your childhood strategy does not have a hugely negative impact on your adult life, but it undoubtedly restricts you in some form. Makes sense, doesn't it? How could a four year old come up with a life strategy that will lead to empowering life responses for an adult?

As we'll see in the next chapters, the eight areas of life are our access points to discovering our own personal survival strategy. But you can also get some insight by asking someone who knows you very well what she sees in you and your behavior, especially in times of conflict or stress. Let me emphasize that this person must be a trusted friend, someone who does not have an agenda or vested interest, someone who is willing to say what she really thinks. What is unconscious to us is often totally obvious to those around us!

Chapter 3: Relationships

Of all the areas of life, relationships are particularly effective at helping us run into ourselves. What can push our hot buttons or trigger our reactions more than the forces at work in a relationship? It's an area that challenges the unique personal survival strategy we created as a child, making it more complex and intricate. As we grow up, we have so many more individuals and situations in our experience to which we need to adapt. We turn our childhood survival strategy into a persona, that false self or face that we present to the world to protect the self inside from harm.

Our very first, most critical relationships are typically with our parents. Our future relationships are based on how we navigated those first, critical relationships. We run into people who are similar to our parents, which triggers our old reactions. Or we encounter people who are different from our parents, which may

cause confusion and uncertainty. Either way, relationships are

perfect access points for revealing personal survival strategies

that have become roadblocks to our growth, as well as exposing

our misunderstandings of the basic principles –

misunderstandings that will also trip us up on the road to

fulfillment. So relationships, as messy, wonderful, uncomfortable,

exciting, and frustrating as they are, become perfect portals for

self-discovery and creating a life of flourishing.

Relationship Defined

In this book, I'm defining relationship as the dynamic or

interaction between two individuals. You also have specific

dynamics with groups like your entire family or your community.

But even if an individual also falls within a larger unit, the energy

exchanged one on one with that individual is different from the

exchange with him or her as a part of the unit. In other words,

your wife is part of your family (the area of Family is discussed in

Chapter 10). But in the area of relationships, we're looking at how you and she relate to each other as individuals, both in public and private, and not just the roles you play in the family unit.

Often we think of relationships as friends and family, maybe including co-workers or people that we know well. But you are in relationship in every single one on one interaction, no matter how fleeting. You have a relationship with the woman at the airport check-in counter and the kid who fills your order at Starbucks, your long-term clients, as well as the person you interviewed for a position in your company that did not get hired. Relationships can last for decades or minutes, but they are still valid energy exchanges that reveal your patterns and barriers to growth.

But often, it's our most intimate relationships that get our attention. A shop clerk can be argumentative and you might forget about it within minutes, probably missing whatever learning that encounter could have provided. But when your spouse or children continually cross you, it's not as easy to ignore. We're almost forced to confront ourselves or risk losing the relationship altogether. It's the same in many relationships on the job. You can walk away from a rude taxi driver, but it's hard to brush off a co-worker who is inconsiderate day in and day out. So our more constant and intimate relationships give us opportunity – and more ammunition – for our self-discovery.

Healthy vs. Unhealthy Relationships

An unhealthy relationship is one that continually triggers childhood traumas and our wired-in reactions to them. In an unhealthy relationship, it's as if our childhood patterns are simply reactivated and replayed. The problem isn't that the pattern was triggered, but that it is not brought to awareness, released, and resolved. Like the movie *Groundhog Day,* it's not that the situations and people are exactly the same. It's that we still react according to old patterns or misunderstandings rather than using circumstance to grow and learn a new type of response.

For instance, a child might have been raised by an alcoholic father who was nonthreatening but also not responsible. That child might grow up and become involved with other men who are similarly irresponsible, maybe her bosses or spouse. She may feel compelled to take care of those men in much the same fashion she felt she had to care for her father. Continuing this childhood survival strategy clearly doesn't serve her as an adult – and it clearly doesn't serve the men that she will not confront.

A healthy relationship on the other hand is one in which there is an equal exchange of energy, a comfortable 'give and take'. Both parties communicate their needs and take 100% responsibility for their responses in the relationship. The two individuals may not be in exactly the same stage of growth, yet they support one another's evolution. Childhood traumas may get triggered but

53

each person is aware – or becomes aware – and takes responsibility for resolving their own childhood survival strategies as well as any misunderstanding of the basic principles that may affect the relationship. At its best, a healthy relationship becomes one of mutual healing and mutual growth.

Romantic Relationships

It is often said that we marry our mother or our father, whichever is the opposite gender parent. To a certain extent, we do this to make sure that we set ourselves up to resolve the original parental issue from our childhood. This trauma or issue has been housed in the unconscious. But by replaying that issue in an adult relationship, we bring it back into our consciousness. It's no longer hidden; it's right in our face again. Often, the childhood survival strategies we used in the past don't quite function in the present. The discomfort this causes gives us the opportunity to reframe and release the issue and old survival strategy by first recognizing it then choosing a different, more life affirming strategy.

For example, if a child is raised by a very domineering and demanding mother, he may seek out a seemingly similar woman to marry. As a child, he knew that a passive/aggressive strategy would keep peace in the household. Initially in his new marriage, he may find comfort in knowing how to deal with his spouse, just like he dealt with his mother. But unless his new spouse had a similar dynamic in her household (dominant mother with passive/aggressive father) and is fully willing to play the same game, odds are that his strategy will no longer function as well as it did as a child. Or, even if his spouse does have the same game going, he may find that he wants more honesty, intimacy and love from a marriage than his passive/aggressive strategy allows him to have.

We also tend to replicate the dynamics we saw in our parents' relationship. If our parents were rarely affectionate and seemed to have no life to themselves behind closed doors, we tend to establish a similar relationship with our own spouse. We assume that what we saw as children is the way that the world works. If we've never seen a truly affectionate, passionate marriage, how would we even know they really exist outside of Hollywood? So we might even unconsciously inherit the survival strategies of our parents and bring them into our own intimate relationships!

Romantic relationships have a lot of charge to them because they involve sex, survival, creating offspring, family connection – all very basic human needs and desires. But other relationships can be points of access to awareness as well.

Other Relationships

Often the friends or co-workers we choose have some striking similarity to family dynamics we experienced as a child. Based on your childhood strategies, you are predisposed to act in a certain way, so you seek complementary energies. For example, a child may have an older brother who demeans and berates her. Later in life, she finds herself consistently choosing employers who treat her the same way, never respecting her work or her worth. If we grew up around people with emotional/mental issues, as adults we may feel that we don't belong with "normal" people – that perhaps they are too boring. The friends we attract are all eccentric, on-the-edge types who provide us the dangerous thrills we experienced as children.

Unless we become conscious of our childhood survival strategies, we usually carry them into our adult relationships. If as kids, we got more attention and felt more powerful by deprecating or bullying our younger siblings, guess what strategy we use in the Boardroom? Or if we received approval for hard work and effort as children, we're likely to become some form of workaholic whether it's in our professional life or the PTA.

The point is not that we don't have flaws. We all do. But when that flaw or weakness becomes dominant, we become one-dimensional. Maybe we work a little too hard or tend to be rough on ourselves and others. The point is, can we stop when that behavior is destructive to those around us and who we really want to be?

Working with the Old Strategies

Your relationship patterns will, to some extent, show up in almost all of your relationships from the casual street corner encounter to the four-decade marriage. But because these patterns are, to a large extent unconscious, it might be tricky to self-identify them.

58

Often it takes a third party, a trusted friend, or even a therapist, to help you see what seems so ingrained.

It's also helpful to pay attention to <u>when</u> you are emotionally triggered; when something sets you off and you find yourself reacting perhaps more vehemently than the situation should warrant. Whenever you feel that automatic, almost beyond your control reaction, pay careful attention. This triggering event and its reaction is an access point. Follow the thread. Does the reaction have an almost déjà vu quality to it? Can you back track and notice other incidents that brought this same reaction up in you? Can you trace it back to something in your childhood? If so, then what?

For most of us, we need to recognize our childhood traumas, reframe, and release them. It's not enough to merely release the trauma and the strategy you created around it. The pattern needs to be replaced with a better, more flexible strategy and awareness.

Your present relationships are perfect opportunities to recreate your future by not following your past. Say, for example, your childhood survival strategy was to run for the hills whenever conflict arose. Today, you're in a relationship that you value but – uh oh! – an argument begins. Everything in your neurology might be telling you to leave, hide, and get the heck out of the situation! But take a deep breath. Is there another option? Every time you choose differently, every time you respond rather than react, you loosen the grip that your old survival strategies have on you.

Now, let's look at how misunderstanding of the basic principles can show up in your relationships.

Perception is Projection

Everything you perceive about someone and every judgment you make about another person is basically the product of your own beliefs and filters. In a relationship, if the two of you don't grasp this, you are essentially two unrealities trying to deal with one another! If we don't understand perception is projection, we assume not only that our beliefs are truth with a capital 'T', but also that everyone else holds the same beliefs! If they are not acting according to these beliefs, well, they must be dishonest, mean, hypocritical, or just plain stupid!

An example: What if you hold the belief that everyone in authority is trying to steal your power? One day, you miss your flight to an important meeting and run into someone at the airline check-in counter with a bit of an attitude. He tells you there's nothing he can do. "You'll have to wait until tomorrow, sir." You come frickin' unglued! Then that idiot on the other side of the counter delivers the ultimate insult: "Just calm down, sir." Calm down! You @#!?!#!! It's as if the guy is trying to emasculate you right there! This teeny, weeny A-hole with the stupid vest is trying to push me into victimhood...

Do you see how it goes? Your belief about authority (and your own sense of powerlessness that you've not yet dealt with) creates an interaction that, in a sense, never happened.

And if your projections affects a 5 minute encounter to that extent, what about your more significant relationships?

Cause & Effect

In life in general, we know that to be empowered and fulfilled, we need to move to 100% at cause for our lives. We need to experience that we are responsible for how we perceive and approach all situations. In relationships, often we try to negotiate that 100% responsibility, wanting to place some of it on the other: "But if he would only communicate better." "Well, if she didn't have so much baggage." In many of our relationships, we are interacting with someone who is not taking 100% responsibility – so why should <u>we</u>?

But there is no negotiating with 100% responsibility for our response to *all* interactions and *all* situations and *all* relationships if we are committed to flourishing. We must be willing to do whatever it takes to build authentic relationships, whether it is with our children or with the bagger at the grocery store – and "doing whatever it takes" does not include changing the other person! It's about changing and growing ourselves. Does that seem like a lot of work? When being 100% at cause becomes a habit, it really isn't. It only feels like a lot of work when we're waffling between *feeling* that we are at the effect of life versus *knowing* that we are at cause.

Creation / Dichotomies

The principle of creation says that whenever you create something, its opposite instantly comes into being. But this is relative on a scale. In other words, if you create something near the mid-point, its opposite will be very close. If you create something on the extreme end of the scale, its opposite will be at the very far opposite end. How does this work in relationships?

If we've chosen an extreme position, we have to create someone in our lives on the other extreme. Remember this phrase? "Can't live with them. Can't live without them." Lovers or enemies we're obsessed with, professional counterparts – haven't we all attached to someone who seemed extremely opposite to us yet we still had a strong attraction? This is the Law of Creation and Dichotomies.

If we stay more toward the middle of the spectrum, we can attract people who are "complementary." They balance us, but in a gentler way. We are not the same but we even each other out, balance one another.

There are two major misunderstandings in this principle that can trip us up in relationships. One is that the balance is static. It isn't. It is a continually moving, fluid balance that is never still. Your spouse is strong, then weaker and you step up accordingly. Your collaborative partner leads the charge then pauses while you take the reins. The balance is in constant movement. The misunderstanding is in thinking that each party of the relationship has a position on the spectrum that is static.

Another misunderstanding is "birds of a feather should stay together." That the uncomfortable rub of differences is wrong. Life is built to intentionally create contrast, and contrast insures movement. When we confine ourselves to relationships with people who are exactly like us, who believe in exactly the same things we believe, who dress like us, talk like us – we lose a major avenue of our growth and fulfillment.

Cycles & Rhythms

With your four selves – physical, emotional, mental, and spiritual – all in their own cycles, it's rare that all are hitting the same point on the cycle at the same time. For example, mentally, you may feel at your sharpest on a particular day, ready to tackle the world and its thorny problems. But on that same day, your physical body might be retreating, wanting rest and quiet to restore itself. If you don't recognize your natural rhythms and cycles, you might wonder, "What's the matter with me? Why am I so tired when I have so much to do?" And if you don't honor these cycles, you might try to push yourself inappropriately by forcing your body beyond its healthy limits, trying to confront emotional issues when your emotions are in flux, or tackling difficult mental challenges when you are not at your best. You can't really do anything about the cycles of your four bodies except be aware of them, honor them, and adjust your behavior as possible around them.

You can't really coordinate the cycles within yourself, much less coordinate them with another person! But the point is not to try and match cycles (though many cycles may fall into synch with those around you) but to be aware of them so you can act accordingly. The trick in this is to pull back far enough from yourself and the other person to observe where you each are in the cycle. In doing so, how to adjust your actions will be more apparent.

For example, if your partner is on a roll mentally and you are also feeling sharp, that may be the time to bring up how you might save up for your child's college education. In this mentally vital mode, the two of you may come up with all kinds of creative ideas. By the same token, if an employee seems to be down emotionally but you are feeling up and excited about the future, this may not be the best time to bring up an exciting new project or even potential promotion.

One of the biggest misunderstandings we have about another's cycles is that we tend to "freeze" our perception of them to a particular point in the cycle. In other words, if a friend is often spiritually aware and awake, we might assume that she is always there. But according to the principle of cycles, she too will have times of "waning" spiritually and will experience doubt, disconnection and confusion that is seemingly uncharacteristic. Your spouse may often be energetic and strong physically. But it's important to not assume that this vibrancy will always be present. Even the most physically fit of us have times when the body needs to rest and restore and not be pushed.

Conscious/Unconscious

The unconscious mind determines about 90% of how we operate in the world. Through a lot of inner work and self-awareness, you can reduce unconscious reactions to around 70%, moving the other 20% into the conscious realm where you can consciously choose your responses and actions. In the dance of relationships, this is particularly important.

We tend to try to be a bit more conscious as well as *unconscious* in on-going, more intimate relationships. We are more unconscious because we are emotionally hooked and that triggers old reactions. But we also may see and consider what we are doing and how we are being in these relationships because there's something at stake. Whether it's a job or a family unit or a friendship, we don't want to lose something so we try a little harder to be our best in the relationship. We may find that our most tender, explosive places are triggered in these relationships.

But still we try harder to keep those reactions under control to avoid the risk of losing what is important to us.

In the "throw-away" relationships, we can really go unconscious and simply act out according to our unconscious patterns. There's not much at stake. However, just because there's not much at stake, we may be able to see the other person more clearly. We can see their jumble of reactions and patterns and notice how these are reflections of our own.

Ecology

The principle of ecology asks, "Is whatever I am doing or who I am being in everyone's best interest?" One of the biggest mistakes in relationships is simply not asking that question. We get so caught up in what we desire and what we need from that relationship that we forget that the person before us has needs, desires, and a path to self-fulfillment as well. Whether it's your boss or your blind date, it's important to consider what you do and how you are taking into consideration the unique needs and desires of the other person.

But what if we don't know the other person well enough to pinpoint what is good for them? Merely pausing and asking the question, taking a moment to try and step into the other person's shoes will give you some insight. So before dismissing that waitress as incompetent, maybe imagine what else she might be handling – stresses at work, at home, bills to pay, aching feet. Is your clever but rude comment really good for her right now? And is it really good for you?

On the flip side, we may also mistakenly assume that the relationship is all about the other person's needs. This is often seen in modern parenting styles. Many of today's parents have become so obsessed with the needs and healthy development of their children that they have placed themselves and their own needs on the back burner. But according to the principle of ecology, if it's not good for you as a parent, it can't be authentically good for the child either. Sometimes it's very healthy for a child to experience that she is not the center of the Universe!

And if your actions are not in everyone's best interest, figure out something else, another option and way of being!

Flexibility

Finding that other option is of course where flexibility comes in. When we are not being run by our unconscious patterns and survival strategies, suddenly we are able to respond to others rather than react. A two year old may throw a tantrum because he doesn't know what he wants or how to get it. Depending on his family, tantrums might be a generalized way of getting something better than what he has.

As adults, we are clearer about the ultimate result we want and more savvy about how to get it. But there can be a major misunderstanding about this newfound adult power, especially in relationships: If we are not applying all of the basic principles, this knowledge may lead us to try and "manipulate" people to get what we want. That is not true flexibility. True flexibility is when we understand and apply the principles and have released and reframed our survival strategies from childhood. At that point, we find that we have many potential avenues to getting what we want and these avenues feel authentic to who we truly are.

Where to Begin

The bottom line in relationships is that your relationship with others will be determined by your relationship with yourself. In the final analysis, there's no one out there but yourself. So to work on your relationships, you must first work on yourself. For many of us, this means find a teacher for whatever our next step may be. There is a classic saying that "The teacher will appear when the student is ready." I think this is true and I also think you need to make sure that the teacher who "appears" does not have his or her own agenda. Personally, I have found that only about 10% of teachers in the personal/spiritual growth arena are really like this. This is one of the reasons we developed FlourishingSummit.com as an online vehicle to find out about different teachers and get recommendations from people you can trust.

I also think that group experiences, workshops, and retreats are very valuable. You find out that you are not alone in the work you need to do within yourself, and you have the benefit of bumping up against others to reflect back to you who you are.

Some of us may need more intensive therapeutic counseling to get to the unconscious patterns that are running (and ruining?) our lives. In finding a therapist, it's also critical to find someone whose own agenda will not interfere with your self-discovery.

Some keys to finding a therapist that is right for you include: 1) Feeling safe and comfortable with that therapist. Therapy is a very vulnerable process and you need to feel safe with it. So it's important that you feel comfortable with and trust your therapist. 2) Knowing your purpose or goal with therapy. Some therapists are comfortable with modifying behaviors but not deeper emotional work. Others are uncomfortable whenever the conversation turns to spirituality. You need to make sure that you and your therapist are on the same page and that your therapist is qualified to go as deeply as you wish to go to be in a safe space to be open. 3) Clear communication. When you are entangled in your patterns, you can't see them. A good therapist can point out what your patterns are and help you to let go of them. Within that process, it's important that you and your therapist can communicate clearly with one another, in a sense, that you speak the same language. It may even help if the two of you have some common life experiences so you can relate to one another.

Chapter 4: Career

Your career is much more than just your job – or it should be. It's more than just how you make a living at any point in time. It's a way of life.

Unfortunately, we've gotten out of thinking of career in this way. Today, the attitude seems to be to grab whatever job you can find and start climbing the ladder of wherever you've ended up. College kids are encouraged to pick majors that will lead to good "job" opportunities. Many of us show up at the job grudgingly on Monday morning then thank God that it's Friday so that we can (hopefully) spend our weekends trying to forget about or recover from whatever we spent most of the week doing.

But for centuries, a person was identified by his career. You were John the Baker or Thomas the Miller, or maybe even Robert the

Smith's son. In pre-industrial societies, free craftsmen (such as textile workers, masons, carpenters, carvers, and glass workers) formed associations based on their trades. Each of these guilds controlled the secrets of their traditionally imparted technology, the arts or mysteries of their crafts. Often your trade was passed on to you by your father and his father before him, and you were a carpenter or a mason no matter what day of the week it was – and you took pride in that fact.

We don't hand our careers down through the generations as often anymore and, sadly, the majority of us no longer take great pride in what we do to make a living. It's just a job. But most of us spend at least a third of our waking hours at "just a job." So shouldn't it be an area where we can thrive and flourish?

Thriving Career

A career that is thriving doesn't necessarily *look* a particular way.

It *feels* a particular way. In other words, you could be a grocery

store bagger and be thriving. Or you could be the most materially

successful real estate mogul in the country and be very unhealthy

in your career. Thriving in career is not measured solely by profit

or prominence. It's the inner qualities that matter.

Answering the following questions will tell you if you are

flourishing in your career:

> *Am I eager to begin my workday, excited to tackle the challenges and enthusiastic about the possibilities it will bring?*
>
> *Do I feel a sense of satisfaction at the end of my workday?*
>
> *Does my work feel like a lifelong pursuit where I can grow and expand as days and years go by?*
>
> *Do I feel that I am called to bring the best of myself to the table? Does this work align with my values and fulfill my passions?*

If you can't answer "Yes!" you might be in the wrong career or have a misunderstanding of the basic principles as applied to career.

Career Designed by Your Survival Strategies

Today, we hear from all directions that we should be "following our passions" when we design a career. But it's a very small percentage of us who ever do that. Why? Because we determine our careers based on the survival strategies we developed as children. For example, if we learned that being seen and not heard was a safe way to navigate our childhood household, odds are that we'd opt to work in accounting rather than as a public speaker. If being "just like Dad" was a way to be safe in the family, we might feel the need to become the doctor, plumber, or minister he was, whether we enjoy those things or not. The daughter who spent most of her childhood trying to cheer up her depressed mother might become a stand-up comic, a

80

psychologist, or a caregiver. The boy who was the go-between keeping peace amongst his siblings might be drawn to diplomacy, negotiations, or tightrope walking!

We also choose careers by the parental and cultural messages we absorbed as children. To survive as children, we learned to look externally for feedback about what we should do or not do— especially in what to do or not do to make a living – rather than internally. We learn these lessons well and they are stuffed into our unconscious. Years later, as we try to figure out what career paths to take, these learnings push us toward certain occupations and away from others.

For example, even the most well intentioned parents prefer that their children be "safe." Some parents emphasize safety so thoroughly that the lesson learned is "Safe is good. Risk is bad." In this case, any occupation that doesn't have 100% job security (which, by the way, has been proven an oxymoron) with pension plans and guaranteed raises and promotions will never be considered. Other parents may highly value artistic endeavors, showing extraordinary support and appreciation for your Crayola creations or violin recitals. If that were the main source of your approval, no matter where your talents lay, you would probably feel more inclined to pursue the artistic life rather than a career in engineering.

Cultural messages also get in the mix to confuse us about the career path we should take. Generally, our culture seems to value professions that require extensive education (attorney, doctor, computer programmer, CPA) and not value careers that emphasize physical labor (contractor, gardener, house cleaner). Our culture also places a lot of emphasis on the amount of money to be made in any career. Becoming a C-Suite executive is considered much more impressive than being a line manager. And within the past few decades especially, celebrity adds prominence to a career. So being an A-List actor (no matter what level of talent) is viewed as more impressive than being a highly skillful character actor on Broadway. Our culture also claims to value professions that make a difference to our world. But oddly, professions that have the most impact on the future of our young people – such as being a teacher or a stay at home parent—get relatively little respect.

Within our overall culture are sub-cultures that have their own particular messages. For example, generally in western culture, being a doctor is seen as more prestigious than being a motorcycle mechanic. But within certain neighborhoods, if you say you want to be a doctor, you'd be an outcast who is considered too hoity-toity and full of yourself. In that same sub-culture, you'd be applauded and respected as a mechanic. In certain sub-sectors of our culture, you will be maligned for becoming a stay at home mother; in others you'd be criticized for being a mother who works outside the home.

As children, we absorb (and sometimes misinterpret) all of these messages. As we begin to think about what our career path should be, these unconscious messages filter through various options and come up with a decision. Or maybe, we don't even have the luxury of giving it any thought at all – we need to grab the first job available just to survive. But even in this "grabbing," what we end up doing has been colored by our childhood survival strategies and parental and cultural messages.

Trouble is that by the time we reach about forty, these motivations become thin. We feel dissatisfied and dead inside. Our "jobs" or our careers may be bringing the bacon home, giving us cultural and parental approval, and fulfilling the demands of our survival strategies, but we've lost ourselves in the process and are certainly not thriving. It doesn't have to be this way. The decision of what to do for a living can be made from a different place, which we'll discuss later in this chapter.

But beyond making the wrong choice in career, we can also block flourishing in a career by our misunderstandings or misuse of the basic principles. The point is to learn the difference between what others want for you and what you truly want for yourself.

Perception is Projection

As in all areas, what we perceive in our work life has little to do with what is there. It has everything to do with the filters through which we are viewing it. In many ways, we never really get away from perception is projection. We will always see through some type of filter. The key to flourishing though is to a) be aware that we are not seeing "the truth" but only seeing through our filters and b) replace filters that are detrimental to our careers with filters that are beneficial. How does this work?

For example, you may notice that you always assume that your bosses are out to get you. You may consistently feel that they are stealing your good ideas and not giving you the credit you deserve. Honestly? If you walk around with that chip on your shoulder, you're bound to be proven right! So how could you reframe that? How could you see this differently? How about: "Wow! What a great lesson in how not to treat employees! This is terrific training for when I get to that level. What else can I learn from him?" Or maybe: "Hmmm. Looks like an opportunity to sharpen my presentation skills so that everyone on the team gets credit."

How about a perception that everyone around you is incompetent and lazy? A social psychologist, Dr. Rosenthal of the University of California, took a group of average children and told their teachers that some of these students were exceptional students while certain others tended to struggle in class and perform poorly. The students that the teachers perceived as promising and intelligent did exceptionally well and achieved very high grades. The others, perceived to be lacking in academic potential, did far worse and many failed for the first time ever! Clearly, our perceptions can have dramatic effect on those around us. What effect would you like to have on your employees or peers?

Cause & Effect

Too many of us fall on the Effect side when it comes to our careers and jobs. Do these lyrics ring a bell? "I owe my soul to the company store." "She works hard for the money and they never treat her right." "I'm taking what they giving 'cause I'm working for a livin'" If you really want to get depressed, just look up all the lyrics from Dolly Parton's *9 to 5*! Except for the entrepreneurs among us, too many of us seem to feel powerless in our careers. It's either the boss man or the workload or the corporate culture that is "doing it to us." Even entrepreneurs often feel that their business runs them rather than the other way around! We end the week exhausted and drained – yet may even work through the weekend just to keep up with this runaway train.

Even if we have chosen a career that is perfect for us, if we stay on the Effect side, we cannot flourish. On the Cause side, we realize that we are responsible for how we feel about our career, how well we decide to do in it, how we relate to our co-workers and subordinates and bosses. From Cause, we recognize that we can stay or leave, work harder or less hard, stress about our performance or not. From Cause, we recognize that we are not only totally responsible for what career we choose but also for our experience of that career.

One of the misperceptions within career is that the career comes first. The job or the company is the important "cause" and we are merely the insignificant, replaceable "effect." Because of this misunderstanding, we have forgotten to take care of ourselves within our work lives. But to truly flourish in career, it's important to follow the direction of every flight attendant: *Be sure to secure your own oxygen mask first before assisting another.* When you experience yourself as totally responsible in your work life, you naturally value yourself and take good care of yourself so you can be effective in what you do.

Creation / Dichotomies

Previously, we discussed the importance of dichotomies in keeping the flow of life going. In the workplace, there are all kinds of dichotomies: projects that create something totally new and others that sustain processes already in place; work that focuses on internal systems and work that engages the external market; big picture plans and focus on minute detail; periods of growth and periods of contraction. Without both sides of the spectrum, businesses will stagnate or implode!

Even if you don't see this kind of diversity in your individual position, you probably still have tasks you love and tasks you don't, work that is easy for you and work that is difficult, projects that are boring and others that excite you. Most importantly, in the workplace, you run into a myriad of people to whom you must relate. You have relationships with "higher ups" and "lower downs," people you enjoy and those you find difficult, people who are similar to you and those who are quite different, people who think and communicate the way you do and those who seem to be from a different planet! In a sense, just as in other relationships, these people all represent parts of you. To have a career that flourishes, you need to recognize these dichotomies, appreciate them for the role they play, and navigate them.

Cycles & Rhythms

What we do for a living is within a much larger energy flow and every part of that flow is important. For example, when we work, we provide something that is of benefit to someone or something else. For that benefit we provide, we receive compensation. In this day and age, that compensation typically comes in the form of money. We use that money to pay for benefits that others provide us (gas for our cars, food for our tables, dental services) so we have another layer of compensation for someone else's work. And so it goes in a chain of giving and receiving.

When this chain is broken or misused, something will have to give somewhere down the line. If I am producing goods or offering services that are of no benefit to others, I don't get compensated. If I pay my utility company but the company refuses to provide electricity to my home, believe me, that chain is going to get upset by an army of my attorneys! In flourishing in our careers, that energy exchange needs to keep moving and stay in balance. The work you do must give a good benefit to another and what you receive must be fair compensation.

Another aspect of cycles and rhythms in career is that each career and each industry has ebbs and flows. Skyrocketing to the top is often a false high. Each step of the ladder or expansion along the way is not just a part of the cycle to put up with until you get promoted or your business moves to the next level. Each stage

has its wisdom and learning to impart. The principle of cycles and

rhythms tells us to keep our eyes open, learn from, and

appreciate every moment of the journey. Especially in today's

economy, the only thing that is certain is change. When we fight

the change of cycles, we tend to shoot ourselves in the foot. But if

we take a deep breath and keep calm, we can ride each cycle's

wave easily.

Conscious/Unconscious

As in all of the areas, our task is to bring what is unconscious in

our careers into our consciousness. When we are conscious of

how our unconscious urges are directing us in our careers, we can

then choose to accept or reject those urges. For many of us, our

work life is especially tied to our self-esteem. This used to be truer

for men than women but now that link has become gender

neutral. We rate our value by what we *do,* not who we *are.* And because of that link, our work life is not just about the contribution we make and the compensation we receive. It also tells us whether we are worthy or not. Ouch!

This connection or link to what we do and how worthy we experience ourselves to be resides in the unconscious and is most often developed in childhood. As a child, we are constantly assessing whether we are valuable enough to be part of the family unit or tribe. Because of that unconscious self-assessment, as adults we often find that attaining our conscious career goals is never enough. That big promotion is satisfying only for a month or so. That bigger paycheck is only thrilling in the first couple of pay periods. Without recognizing and coming to terms with your unconscious attitudes about self-esteem, you find yourself never satisfied and never expressing who you really are in the workplace.

But once we unearth those unconscious messages and release their grip on us, we're often more able to step into a career that allows us to express our true selves. This is how I define a flourishing career. It's one where you feel a sense of showing up to do what you love to do. As Confucius said, "Choose a job you love and you will never have to work a day in your life."

Ecology

Fortunately, our culture is beginning to appreciate the importance of ecology in career. Your career needs to be good for everyone: you, your family, your community, your world. Clearly, we've seen how ignoring ecology in career and business does not work. The old culture of "the ends justifies the means" as in the TV show *Mad Men* proved to be a disaster when investment bankers applied it to their dealings on Wall Street in the first years of the 21st century! Profit is not "king" but just one of the pieces in the puzzle.

Today, it's encouraging that many companies are supporting work/life balance. These companies finally understand that the organization will be healthier if its employees are happy about themselves and their home lives. They are aware that the work environment must support physical and mental well-being, and they understand that employees need the opportunity to bring energy back to their spouses and children at the end of the day. These cutting-edge companies (some of which have been around for generations) also recognize that they must be good community partners and global citizens to thrive, which is evident in their emphasis on community service and green practices.

Just as forward thinking companies are honoring ecology, each of us must pay attention to our individual ecology. A promotion to a managerial level may sound good from an income perspective, but the extra hours may not be healthy for your family if you have young children to raise. Dropping your teaching gig at the high school to become a vagabond artist may satisfy some personal need, but is it a good move income-wise? Does the widget you

want to make have negative repercussions on the water system?

If so, is there another way to produce it?

Flexibility

As we've noted in other chapters, flexibility is really a by-product

of uncovering and reframing our unconscious childhood survival

strategies and the parental and societal messages we absorbed.

When we aren't restricted by those strategies and messages, we

are totally free to choose, not only what occupation to pursue,

but also how we approach any career path we choose.

The following questions will help you determine your current level

of flexibility as it relates to career:

Make a long list of all kinds of occupations from
candlestick maker to nuclear physicist, janitor to President
of the United States, opera star to computer programmer.

*Are there any that you absolutely **cannot** do? Why? Who says so?*

If you had all the talent and training required for that job, could you do it? Would you want to? Why or why not? Who says so?

Are there any jobs on that list that are particularly good or bad jobs? Why? Who says so?

If most of those career options seem possible – not necessarily probable! – then you have a fair amount of flexibility in your career choice. (And the "Who says so?" question should help flush out some of those unconscious messages.)

Now, let's check your flexibility in your current career:

Thinking about your current career, do you have the option to work harder or less hard? Why or why not? Who says so?

Could you see yourself reaching a higher level in this career? Could you see yourself stepping down a few notches in this career? Why or why not? Who says so?

Can you interact with your clients, co-workers, subordinates, or bosses differently than you've done up until now? Why or why not? Who says so?

Could you do whatever you do in a totally different way than you have up until now? Why or why not? Who says so?

As in all areas of life, the degree of your flexibility determines your power and effectiveness in career.

Finding Your Perfect Work

Some people seem to know exactly what career they want from the time they're in diapers! They pursue this career and find rich satisfaction. But I'd say that's less than 10% of us. The rest of us have to figure it out at some point. It would be great if as young people, we were taught how to really determine the perfect career for ourselves! But many of us have already spent decades in careers that we chose simply because they had the potential to pay well. But no matter where you are, it's never too late to change course and find the career path that will help you flourish

fully.

You begin by recognizing your passions. Some of us have never

even considered what we're passionate about so this may feel like

a stretch. But sit yourself down and brainstorm about all the

things you are passionate about. Don't concern yourself with how

that passion might translate into a practical lifelong pursuit.

Simply write down whatever comes to you. And don't just think

about it, write it down. The very exercise of writing will keep you

focused.

When you feel like you have an exhaustive list of passions, leave it

alone for a few days to let your unconscious process it. When you

come back to the list, cross out anything you noted that doesn't

seem very important and circle passions that seem particularly

important. Next, write down your values like freedom, flexibility,

security. Again, write as many as you can. Then leave your list for a few days, come back to it and cross out any values that seem less important and circle those that are most important.

Your passions and values are telling you who you *are* in life. Only now are you ready to figure out what you want to *do* in life. Looking at these two lists, what possible career paths fit into them? Brainstorm about all the possibilities and write them down. You may want to bring in a friend at this point to help you broaden your career possibilities.

When you have a few that seem to fit for you, begin your research. Use the internet and your contacts to find out what these careers really look like. How much education is needed? What measures success in these occupations? What lifestyle do these careers create? After you've weighed it all, it's time for a test drive!

In my experience, the only way to really know if a career is right for you is to try it out in some form. I wish job or career descriptions could come with a warning label as on a prescription bottle listing all the hidden side effects of that career! But they don't. You'll only find out if the occupation is full of people who aren't compatible with you or the hours are too ridiculously long or the work too repetitive by testing the waters. So whether it's becoming an apprentice or taking a temp job in that occupation, see if you can get your feet wet before jumping in totally.

If you really follow your passion and honor your values, the emotional ups and downs that come with any lifelong pursuit will seem minor and totally manageable.

Chapter 5: Health & Fitness

Your body is the sacred vessel that houses your consciousness. As such, don't you think it deserves a little respect?

Until fairly recently, taking care of our physical health through diet and exercise was not a dominant interest in our culture. By the middle of the twentieth century, three martini lunches (or six-packs after work), smoking to look cool, and eating whatever we pleased had become almost the norm for many adults. Parents made sure that their offspring ate their carrots and spinach, but seemed to abandon nutrition for themselves. And exercise? Why walk when you could drive? Why get up and turn the channel when you have a fancy remote to do it for you? Why trudge up those stairs when elevators and escalators could lift you effortlessly?

But in the past couple of decades, we've started to notice the toll

this kind of lifestyle has taken on us. So we join gyms, count our

calories, and wear nicotine patches. We search the web for the

next greatest nutritional supplement or perfect exercise routine.

We measure our cholesterol, our waistlines, and our blood

pressure. But is that really what health is about? Are we chasing

health from the wrong direction?

Interconnectedness of Our Bodies

The physical body is in a sense only one of our "bodies."

According to Huna and other spiritual teachings, we also have a

spiritual body, a mental body, and an emotional body. The

spiritual body, or consciousness, is the most powerful of the four

and the most simple. It is the One and the source of all that

follows. In some practices, the physical body is seen as something

to conquer, to overcome. Personally, I think that is a

misunderstanding. We were born into our bodies for a reason. It's the vehicle by which we can navigate material existence and therefore learn all that this plane can teach us. Without it, where are we? Just as we take care of our cars so they will continue to get us where we want to go, we need to care for our bodies.

Our mental body is the next most powerful. "As we think, so shall it be." "Thoughts in mind produce after their kind." "Mind over matter." Unfortunately, in terms of physical health, some of us have taken that "mind over matter" to an extreme. Mentally, we feel strong and eager to attain certain goals, so we drive our bodies farther than they should be driven. We ignore the body's signals until those signals have progressed to debilitating disease.

Our emotional body also has a strong, and sometimes not positive, impact on the body. It's now common knowledge that allowing our emotions to stay in a stressed or angered or depressed state does incredible harm to our physical bodies. Through the cortisol, these emotions releasing is meant to have positive effects (a quick burst of energy for survival reasons, heightened memory functions, a burst of increased immunity, lower sensitivity to pain). But when we hold on to negative emotions, that constant flow of cortisol becomes toxic. Repercussions include impaired cognitive performance; suppressed thyroid function; blood sugar imbalances such as hyperglycemia, decreased bone density, decrease in muscle tissue, higher blood pressure, and lowered immunity; and inflammatory responses in the body. To top it off, unhealthy amounts of cortisol are connected to increased abdominal fat, which is associated with heart attacks and strokes!

Our physical bodies are the most complex, yet least powerful of our bodies. Yet, the impact flows not only downward from other bodies to the physical, but also upward from our physical bodies to our other bodies. For example, studies have shown that high consumption levels of sugar-containing soft drinks were associated with mental health problems among adolescents even after adjustment for other factors. Exposure to food additives in children has been implicated in the induction and severity of behavioral disorders such as attention deficit hyperactivity disorder (ADHD).[1] Several recent experiments conducted with adults show that exercise performed on a regular basis for several weeks alters brain functions. Physical activity results in several biological responses in muscles and organs, which, in turn, modify and regulate the structure and functions of the brain.[2] So doing physical things to increase our level of physical health directly affects our emotional and mental health.

Flourishing in Health & Fitness

Flourishing in our physical health and fitness requires the participation of all of our other bodies. To promote health in our physical bodies, we need to be healthy and balanced in our

---

[1] http://www.feingold.org/Research/adhd.html#Lien2006

[2] http://www.ncbi.nlm.nih.gov/pmc/articles/PMC2748863/

spiritual, mental, and emotional bodies as well. We need to cultivate a respect for our physical bodies and treat them with at least as much care as we would a precious pet! Just as our bodies serve us as the sacred vessel of our consciousness, we need to serve them by being good stewards.

The definition of good health and fitness also is dependent upon the unique mission we determine for our own lives. For example, if my mission is to be a high-performing athlete to show others that we can break through seemingly impossible barriers by setting new world records, clearly I need to cultivate an extraordinary level of health and fitness. But if my mission is to be a writer and craft novels that inspire and entertain, my level of health and fitness will be different – though even in this seemingly sedentary lifestyle, good health and fitness will be important to fulfill on the mission I've set for myself.

Once we know what good health and fitness looks like for ourselves, what gets in the way? As in the other areas of life, our childhood survival strategies and misunderstandings of basic principles can lead us down an unhealthy path physically.

How Childhood Survival Strategies Come into Play

Before the age of six or seven, most of us do not have critical faculties that are mature enough to make good decisions for ourselves. Our caretakers are primarily responsible for caring for our bodies, the level of exercise we're encouraged or allowed to do and the food we eat. So we eat what's put in front of us, what tastes good and feels good. But as we develop our survival strategies, food can become a large component.

For example, many of us grew up with the Clean Plate Club, exhorted by our parents to "finish our meals" often with the added guilt of "remember the starving children in India." Wasting food became the cardinal sin. To be "good" and retain our parents' approval, we began a lifetime of eating more than our bodies really wanted. By the time we're adults and this strategy is unconscious, we wonder why we can't seem to push ourselves away from the dinner table when we've had enough.

Certain foods – such as processed foods, refined sugars, and other simple carbohydrates – also have a numbing effect. If we are not able to receive reassurance from our parents or environment, we seek the relief of emotional numbness these foods can cause. We "stuff" our emotions by stuffing our faces with junk food. We've learned to call these "comfort foods." And though it's the survival strategy we devised as children, as adults responding to sadness or disappointment with comfort food in our culture is so prevalent that it's almost considered an acceptable response!

A passive/aggressive strategy developed in childhood can also result in such eating disorders as bulimia and anorexia.

Sometimes all a child feels that she can control in life is what she will allow to go into her mouth or stay in her stomach. Or if a child feels he can only gain attention when he is in distress, he may use illness or hurt himself in "accidents" to get the love he craves. The primal desire to fit in causes many of us to be obsessive and addictive in working out beyond healthy limits. Teenage girls obsess about being fat and assume that boys won't like them (and therefore, they will not find a mate, which is a basic survival urge). Many of these young women not only starve themselves, but also punish their bodies with aggressive long workouts on malnourished bodies. Though the initial intention was to feel and look better, many hurt themselves and would be better served by learning to accept who they are.

Bottom line is that your patterns of taking care of your body – or not – often reveal your childhood survival strategies that have become unconscious. Misunderstandings or misuse of the basic principles also impact physical health and fitness.

Perception is Projection

One of the first western medical doctors to appreciate the concept of perception is projection was a plastic surgeon named Dr. Maxwell Maltz. Dr. Maltz wrote a book in 1960 called *Psycho-Cybernetics* in which he discussed how we simply do not see our physical selves as they are. He tells several poignant stories of patients who received extensive plastic surgery only to see the same reflection in the mirror they saw before the work was done.

Today, our perception of our bodies is highly tainted by the gleaming teeth, rippling abs and slender thighs of television and movie celebrities. Remember when not all performers had straight teeth? When not all models were size zero and not all talk show hosts had perfect hair? Too many of us look in the mirror and see what *isn't* (when compared to current cultural trendsetters), not what *is*. And we base our actions on what we "see." For example, an anorexic child will continue to "see" herself as chubby in the mirror, even when she is skin and bones. Because this is what she "sees," she refuses to eat and fears gaining weight.

Cause & Effect

There are a couple of misunderstandings when it comes to health and the principle of Cause & Effect. The first misunderstanding is denying that what we do to and for our bodies has a direct impact on our physical health. There are some things beyond our control. For example, how tall we are, our race, our gender, our age. But we are totally responsible when it comes to the food we put into our bodies and how we use (or abuse) them. We can't smoke three packs a day and expect to have vibrant lungs. We can't live a sedentary life and expect to be muscular. We can't overeat or under-nourish our bodies and expect peak performance physically. A person who is totally on the Cause side of life doesn't complain that her work hours prevent her from exercising or that her limited food budget means she can't buy healthy foods.

Another misuse of Cause & Effect is the attitude of falling *victim* to disease or other physical challenges. Physical issues are not "out to get you" or any kind of personal attack. The issues in themselves do not make our lives miserable. It's how we choose to relate to them that determines how we feel.

A young South African named Nkosi contracted AIDS at birth. But through his short life, he chose to live his life actively supporting others with AIDS. At age 11, he gave an impassioned speech at an International conference appealing for an end to ignorance about the illness and violent discrimination against those with the disease. Nkosi was awarded the Nobel Children's Prize for Peace posthumously.

How many of these stories have we heard? Where an illness or a physical challenge is used as a launch pad for a greater purpose or message? Nkosi and others like him epitomize being on the Cause side of their own lives.

Creation / Dichotomies

Whenever we create something, its opposite comes into being. In terms of our physical health and fitness, the key is to notice the extremes. For example, a strict, minimal calorie diet to lose weight often sets up a strong dichotomy that begs for its opposite: a binge. Yo-yo dieters understand this effect. On the other hand, a diet that is more moderate, that stays near the center of the teeter-totter, will not evoke a strong opposite.

Seemingly positive physical activities can also be extreme. Take the example of the body builder who becomes so muscular he cannot touch his own shoulder! Or the marathon runner who trains so heavily that she becomes infertile. Our physical bodies are healthier when in a balanced state of moderation rather than an extreme, whether it concerns diet or exercise.

Cycles & Rhythms

The biggest misuse of this principle is when we try to thwart the natural cycles and rhythms of our bodies. One of the most basic of physical cycles is activity and rest. Our bodies need both activity and rest to be healthy. We have natural waking and sleeping cycles that, when honored, give us a natural balance of energy. But too many of us try to pack in 80-hour workweeks and hectic social lives —not to mention average 5 hours of television we watch every day – which leaves inadequate time for the sleep we need. It's true that not everyone needs the 8 hours of sleep our mothers told us we needed each night. But many of us feel constantly fatigued. It's not surprising that the Centers for Disease

Control and Prevention reports that over a third of us have

symptoms of sleep deprivation.[3]

Another natural cycle is that of aging. Somewhere during the last

century, our culture decided that to remain ever young was the

goal. Rather than appreciating and revering our elders and the

wisdom they have to offer, we started worshipping at the altar of

youth. Plastic surgeons are making a bundle so we can look

younger. Medications and supplements promise to give us back

our adolescent vitality and sexual prowess. We struggle to keep

up with the latest style trends, technologies, and innovations.

Of course, not all of this is bad. Aging gracefully doesn't have to

mean allowing ourselves to become decrepit. But when we deny

or fight the natural process of aging in our bodies, when we

continually try to recapture the bodies of our youth, we miss the

learning of our body's natural cycles. Our body is a wonderful

---

[3] http://www.cdc.gov/Features/dsSleep/

machine. It takes the bruising and battering we put upon it and still continues to work. However, lack of attention toward our bodies causes sickness and disease to arise, exhaustion to take over, and an overall a lack of energy. Resting and "rebooting" our bodies is just as important as a healthy workout each day. Whatever strain (good or bad) we put on the body, we need to allow for that same amount of recharge to create a balanced lifestyle.

Conscious/Unconscious

Functions of the body are regulated by the unconscious mind, and the unconscious mind is highly skilled at its job. However, as mentioned earlier, childhood survival strategies and cultural messages hidden in the unconscious will directly affect how the unconscious directs the body.

For example, the unconscious is responsible for determining threat and directing the body to activate survival mechanisms. But the unconscious may classify people or situations as threatening that really are not. If your heart starts pounding the moment you see a circus clown, you know that your unconscious is giving your body an unnecessary danger signal. You can make the conscious decision to work with your unconscious and correct its misperception of the situation.

Ecology

The area of health and physical fitness, even more obviously than the other areas, must fit ecologically into your entire lifestyle – and those around you. Your health choices affect your family, your community, and ultimately your world. How? A Dear Abby column years ago gave the example of a woman who refused to wear her seatbelt. A head-on collision left her totally paralyzed when she flew through the window. Her husband, who was the passenger and wearing his seatbelt, ended up with a few cracked ribs. But for the remainder of her life, he and her children had to care for her, using all of their life's savings to handle her medical bills. When their money ran out, taxpayers started footing the bill through welfare and Social Security. Her health decision (to not wear her seatbelt) had impacts far beyond her own life.

We may feel that our bodies are our own business. But our lives are fully interconnected. Take the issue of obesity. In the US, two thirds of our population falls into the overweight category with one third of our population falling into the obese category (which is a BMI of over 30). Medical costs for an obese person average 42% higher than a person within the normal weight range. In 1998, $78.5 Billion per year was spent on healthcare (50% financed by Medicare and Medicaid). From 1998 to 2006, obesity increased by 37% and the cost of this increase was an additional $40 Billion *per year* to our annual healthcare costs. An individual's decision to become or to stay obese does not just impact his own life. It is part of the entire ecology of our broader community.

Flexibility

As in other areas of life, flexibility in health and physical fitness comes naturally when childhood survival strategies and cultural and familial messages that have been unconscious come to light and are dealt with. While they are still unconscious, these strategies and messages run our lives and certainly our decisions and actions regarding our bodies. Though we may consciously know that some of our choices are not healthy, we feel powerless to make the changes we want because these strategies and messages are wired into our neurology.

The truth is that we <u>do</u> have the ability to have a healthier body no matter how hopeless it seems! We may not be able to stretch a 5'1" frame into a 5'10" frame, but we can definitely have enormous impact on the shape, vitality, and health of the body we do have. But if we don't tackle our unconscious messages to ourselves ("My whole family has big thighs, so I will always have them." "Losing weight is a struggle." "I'm too old to get back in shape."), it will always feel like an uphill climb. We'll be using our conscious to battle against imbedded unconscious messages that are now affecting our very physical chemistry.

To gain flexibility in this area and give ourselves more options for how we behave and feel, we need to get our unconscious to partner with us toward our conscious goals. We do this by first uncovering those unconscious messages that thwart our attempts toward health. What do we tell ourselves about health? Exercise? Eating? Are these messages *really* true? Where do we feel urges that are counter to what we would like to do health-wise? For example, that urge to polish off a plate of brownies, where did it come from?

After this self-inquiry, the next step is to re-wire the unconscious mind's negative messages so that it is in alignment with the positive outcomes that we want. Methods like neuro-linguistic programming or hypnosis can be very effective for this. In doing this, we want to make sure that our health goals are *our* goals, not just the goals of the media (i.e. to be pencil thin or have six-pack abs!) or the goals of our friends or family. And, we want to fully accept what we cannot change in our bodies, like our height or age.

Specific Practices

I don't claim to be a health & fitness guru but there is an incredible amount of information available on the subject. In the past several decades, physical well-being has become a focal point with plenty of research to study and numerous approaches to consider. I've done my own research and come to conclusions that are appropriate for my own physical health and fitness. You'll need to do the same. While doing your investigation, consider these suggestions.

First, always listen to your own body. Whether it's a prescribed medication or an exercise routine, by tuning in to your own body, you will know what is right for you. Second, check out the credibility and longevity of whatever diet or exercise plan you consider. Is it a flash-in-the-pan fad or is there some solid foundation to it? Is someone just trying to sell you something or are you being offered support, guidance, and measures of success?

Chapter 6: Spirituality

What's the old saying? Never discuss religion or politics. But spirituality (which is quite different from religion) is a hot topic today. "Man's search for meaning" has hit the headlines. From the *New York Times* to Oprah's *O Magazine,* the mainstream media is responding to the cravings of John Q Public by discussing, analyzing, and commenting on our spiritual nature. Maybe it's a reaction to our world, which has become increasingly difficult, confusing, and volatile in every way from the weather to the economy. Or maybe it's just a new stage of our evolution or the advent of quantum physics, but everyone – from corporate leaders to physical therapists –seems to be referring to our spiritual nature.

What Spirituality is Not

I mentioned that spirituality is not religion. Religion is a manmade construct. In my mind, it is the attempt by a few to control the many by positioning themselves as a conduit to God. The rules of various religions were often created in response to conditions of the time in which they were conceived, such as not mixing meats with dairy (which may have hygienic validity). Some religions were created in reaction to other religions, such as Protestantism as a reaction to the Catholic Church. But even though every religion has a mystical, more esoteric side that relates more to true spirituality, many of us have found that adhering to the traditional fundamentals of any particular religion can thwart rather than assist our attempts to flourish in the area of spirituality.

Maintaining control over our behavior is becoming more and more difficult for religions. In Western culture, going to church every Sunday (or to synagogue for the Sabbath) is not as

126

mandated as it was generations ago. And we are exposed to more varied beliefs than ever before through travel and immigration, television, the internet, and social media.

When I attended Catholic school as a youngster, people always told me "Don't go to a non-Catholic school or you'll lose your religion." In my case, this turned out to be true. When I was no longer surrounded by the rules and regulations of the church on a daily basis, I started to question and reject Catholicism. I think this happens to many of us when we are no longer encased in the religion of our youth. The good news is that when we turn from the religion of our childhood, we often feel a void, a sense of something missing. It is this sense of something missing that can motivate our quest for true spirituality. As Lenny Bruce said, "Everyday, people are straying away from the church and going back to God."

Materialists

There is a religion that many don't recognize as such and that is the "religion" of materialism or scientism. This religion states that nothing is valid that cannot be experienced through the five physical senses. To me, this seems the height of hubris. So the world was flat before we could "see" or prove that it was a sphere? As our scientific tools become more sophisticated and we are able to observe the "God particle" at work, many materialists are finding it hard to deny the existence of a power they cannot experience with these five senses. But the five senses are designed strictly for the physical plane and that's the only place they operate effectively. The five senses cannot capture the spiritual. On the physical plane, we utilize our five senses to "prove" what is real and what isn't. When dealing with the spiritual plane, you must go beyond your five senses.

Spirituality

Most religions discourage questioning and emphasize the fixed answers that make up their canons. But true spirituality begins with a question: Who am I really? Via this question, we begin to access our intrinsic personal connection to Divinity. We've had it all along – we were just unconscious of it. We come to the physical plane so that we can return to our spiritual nature consciously.

As defined by most religions, God is a being that acts like a somewhat capricious human (judging harshly, doling out gifts arbitrarily, creating laws for his own pleasure). But in true spirituality, God is not a thing or a being, but consciousness itself. It is everything and everything is God. Because the word God is often charged with old images of a white-haired guy sitting on a throne waiting to punish us, personally I prefer to use the word Divinity.

129

Everything in creation originates from Divinity, the spiritual level of being. It moves through the mental, emotional levels until it is finally made manifest in the physical. The spiritual level is very simple: it is all one. At the physical level, everything appears complicated as the "10,000 things" Daoists talk about. But as we begin to awaken, we realize that we are part of the One and the One is within us. This journey and experience is the beginning of flourishing in spirituality.

Childhood Survival Strategies and Spirituality

For many of us, God was the ultimate "parent" that we had to please. Many of us remain attached to the religions of our childhood in this child-like manner without delving more deeply into the esoteric teachings beneath most religions. This attachment to our childhood understandings of religion keeps us stuck in our spiritual growth.

Typically, the survival strategies we use with our parents are replicated in our relationship with God or Divinity. If we chose to be passive/aggressive with our parents, we might do the same with our God. For example, the "perfect" altar boy might be the kid who steals communion wine when no one is looking! If you chose to be compliant and obedient to get approval from your parents, you might be unquestioning and dutiful in your religious practice as well. By following the thread of how you relate to the religion of your childhood, you can identify your childhood survival strategies and begin to dismantle them when they no longer serve you.

What about those of us who were raised with no religion? We still had beliefs about religion or God instilled in us by our families, our communities, and our culture. And we still developed survival strategies toward the religions around us. For example, many atheist families taught their children that belief in a higher power is merely a lack of character or strength. Other families with no particular religious affiliation taught their children that God was a mysterious, unknowable being so there was no point in trying. Whatever the belief – and especially if it can be stated in a black and white manner – it remains an obstacle to flourishing in spirituality until it is brought to light and examined.

Perception is Projection

Many of our basic beliefs are, in a sense, spiritual in nature. As Albert Einstein famously said, "The most important decision we make is whether we believe we live in a friendly or hostile universe." It's clear how the assumption the universe or life itself is "friendly" can impact our lives. We see every obstacle as a helpful lesson, every relationship as a gift toward our good. It's equally clear how the belief that life itself is "hostile" can impact our perception: Every blip in the road becomes a punishment; every relationship a potential threat to our survival.

Also, despite what materialists might believe, we perceive on many levels, and not just through the five senses. Spirituality is

132

based on an inner knowing or sensing that may be unfamiliar to many of us. We live in a world that focuses on the five senses so our intuitions or that still small voice of the Divine may not seem "real" as they begin. Even as our inner knowing becomes stronger, we still have the filters of the unconscious that color or distort its message.

Quantum physicists are beginning to acknowledge the presence of consciousness. For example, Dr. Amit Goswami, a theoretical nuclear physicist at the University of Oregon, has written extensively about consciousness and the interrelationship of mind, matter, and divinity. In his book, *God is Not Dead*, Dr. Goswami says we need to break through our materialistic perceptual conditioning, a reality that was defined by Newtonian physics, and adopt a quantum view to truly understand and experience consciousness and God.

Cause & Effect

In many religions, you can become the effect of a vengeful and capricious God. There's a certain solace in saying that "It's all in God's hands" as if God is something other than yourself. But on a true spiritual path, we are always on the cause side of the equation. We are not separate from this Divinity that is all things – therefore, there can be no other cause than us.

A spiritual misinterpretation of the basic principle of Cause & Effect is in the way the Law of Attraction is used. Somehow, that law has been interpreted to say that "you will attract what you really want – if you want it badly enough." The Law of Attraction works 100% of the time. But its real directive is that "you attract who you *are*," not just what you want. In this sense, you truly are at Cause at all times, attracting various conditions and effects to yourself that are very appropriate for who you are being.

Creation / Dichotomies

In the realm of spirituality, a dichotomy that is often presented is true power versus force. Force is in the external, such as the control that governments use to compel others to behave and believe in a certain way. But true power is the internal alignment to the Divine within. Power tends to be quiet, calm, and steady, whereas force is often loud, excitable, and sporadic. Force has needs and hungers; spiritual power does not. Along the spiritual path, it is not uncommon for someone to tap true power then focus it externally where it becomes force. It is often the misuse of a spiritual power that turns into a religion or cult.

Cycles & Rhythms

As in all areas, there is a cyclical nature to the spiritual path. There are learning curves, times of confusion and overwhelm, that lead to times of understanding and centeredness – only to become confusion and overwhelm again. This is often misunderstood as some kind of problem along the spiritual path. We "had it" but now we think we "lost it." Unlike a religion, where you can "get it" relatively quickly, absorb specific teachings, and know you are set for life, the spiritual path is more winding and less clear-cut because it is a unique, individual path that each of us must take.

Spiritual vision and experience follows a certain rhythm in each of us that cannot be rushed, no matter how dedicated and eager we are. This is why weekend spiritual retreats and workshops, while helpful as a beginning, cannot deliver the entire package of spiritual empowerment. The insights gained in these gatherings need time to ripen in experience, to become integrated into our lives. We understand these insights at one level – then find ourselves cycling through an entirely new level of understanding. "Instant enlightenment" might sound attractive but that isn't how spirituality typically unfolds. The natural cycles and rhythms of our unfolding allow the other parts of ourselves to become ready and grounded for our full empowerment.

136

Conscious/Unconscious

The purpose of life is to return to our spiritual nature consciously. To do this, we need to engage our unconscious mind as well. In many spiritual teachings, including Huna, the unconscious mind has an important part to play in our spiritual unfoldment. The unconscious mind is the conduit for the conscious mind, which cannot directly access the Higher Self or Divine.

In traditional religions, emphasis is placed on conscious acts of prayer or worship. But the real power is with the unconscious connection. Experience of spiritual connection may be motivated by a conscious decision but the connection itself is more of an "allowing" process. In other words, rather than demanding that the Divine show Its face, a spiritual seeker surrenders and allows that connection to be.

This is where mediation can be essential. Allowing yourself to be in a meditative state lets the unconscious mind settle and connect with the Higher Self and the Divine. We have come to believe that

"seek and ye shall find" or "knock and the door shall be opened"

is what we need to do, when in fact the simplest act of being is

where true connection lies. You can look everywhere, uproot

every tree, and turn over every stone. But looking does not lead

to finding. Allowing does. It is when we accept and allow that we

find the answers we seek and the connections we desire.

Flexibility

As in all areas, flexibility is the natural result of uncovering

childhood survival strategies and messages in the unconscious

that drive our behaviors and perceptions. Once these unconscious

imperatives are brought to light, we have the option to dismantle

them and make other choices. Flexibility is particularly important

in creating a flourishing spiritual life. Why? Because the spiritual

path itself is not a tight, defined structure that can be quantified

and packaged. Discovering and cultivating that inner connection with the Divine requires patience as well as the ability to think, feel, and act differently than you may have done previously. The ineffable is just that: indescribable. As Ayn Rand wrote, "God... a being whose only definition is that he is beyond man's power to conceive."

Also, an obstacle to flourishing spiritually can be when we find a good path but become attached to it. Rather than doing the deep internal work required of a spiritual path, we cling to its particular practices or rituals. Or we hit our comfort zone within it and stay stuck rather than moving to a new path. To find fulfillment spiritually, we must continually do a "gut check" and ask ourselves honestly whether we are continuing to grow and expand. If the answer is "no," it may be time to move on.

Ecology

When we are fully aligned with our Higher Self, all else falls into place. Any action we take will automatically be good not only for ourselves personally but also ultimately good for our families, our community, our country, our planet. Since everything is One, it can be no other way. That's the good news.

The trick is that before we get to that state of being, while we're still trying to connect to our inherent connectedness, ecology is not necessarily automatic. Should we judge potential spiritual paths by how ecological they are? Perhaps. But if a path demands that we deny our families, reject our communities and do harm to our country or our planet, perhaps it's not a path we should consider.

Finding the right path does initially take some seeking. But seekers who are sincerely on the path often find that "when the student is ready, the teacher will appear." We recognize our right teachers and paths in different ways. But asking whether the path is ecological is a good place to start.

Specific Practices

There are a myriad of spiritual practices that can lead us toward spiritual fulfillment. My favorite is:

Gratitude: Present in almost all paths is the attitude of gratitude. Meister Eckhardt said that if the only prayer you pray is "Thank You, God," that will be enough. Many teachers advise making gratitude lists upon waking and before you go to sleep, placing your focus firmly on what you *do* have in your life, not on what you *don't* have. I like to thank the Divinity, my unconscious mind and my Higher Conscious Mind for all my blessings, large and small. The tipping point that allows your connectedness to feel more present is when you find yourself in a state of appreciation much more consistently than concern or complaining.

Spiritual practices will begin to occur naturally as you progress on your own spiritual path. Many people choose bits from one path and bits from another. Whatever brings you to that conscious connection of your intrinsic spiritual nature is perfectly

acceptable.

Chapter 7: Personal Growth & Development

Personal growth and development is really based on the evolutionary imperative that demands that we keep expanding beyond who we have been. In a flourishing life, this growth is continuous and covers all parts of us, from our skill sets to our emotional intelligence. We enter the world with a certain set of understandings, talents, abilities, and inclinations. Our charge is to continually nurture and expand upon what we've been given. In other words, personal growth and development is all about change.

As John F. Kennedy said, "The only unchangeable certainty in life is that nothing is unchangeable or certain." Personal growth is about embracing change and growth, not waiting for it to happen to you.

Life Long Learning

Many people assume that the main learning in life is in our youth. We dutifully go through school to acquire basic knowledge. We hone our personas so we can navigate our relationships. We learn a trade or profession so we can support ourselves. But after that, except for some on-the-job training, many of us figure the learning process is done. By our mid-twenties, many of us no longer seek to stretch and explore. We figure that we're fully developed adults, no longer works in progress. We've arrived.

But staying within that box is not what a flourishing life is about. In nature, once you stop growing, you start dying. And with life expectancies in this country becoming longer, 60 plus years of dying is much too long! To truly flourish and find fulfillment, we must become life-long learners, constantly pursuing opportunities to expand our horizons, grow in our intellectual understandings, and deepen our emotional capacity.

144

Learning is not necessarily about pursuing degrees or credentials. This may be a natural result of life-long growth, but it isn't the goal. Letters after your name will not bring lasting satisfaction. It's the learning that those letters represent that is important, and that learning can act as a launch pad for further discoveries and expansion.

It's also not necessarily about chasing down gurus or seminars. Experiences designed to encourage your growth are an important part of the picture. But running from workshop to workshop is not where the real expansion happens. It's in doing the internal work that these workshops and trainers teach. True growth happens when you apply your learnings to your life. When you do this, you find that life itself provides plenty of opportunities for growth and expanded awareness. And if your environment doesn't encourage that growth, you may need to change environments.

The Role of Childhood Strategies

The basic urge to evolve and grow is almost in direct opposition to the basic imperative to survive! Even when we find ourselves caught in survival strategies that don't feel good, we often still prefer them over the change that personal growth demands. How many of us stay in poor relationships or dead-end jobs? We do so because we are more comfortable with the misery we know rather than risk a misery we may not be able to cope with. For example, you may have unearthed your passive/aggressive strategy as a child. And though it worked well with your parents, you now know consciously that this strategy is causing your marriage to be less than happy. But even with this knowledge, even having tools and resources to help you create a change, your unconscious mind (which is primarily responsible for your basic survival) will resist making this change at all costs! It argues that your marriage may not be happy, but what if change causes it to

146

implode? What if you let these defenses down and your spouse attacks while you are vulnerable? What if, what if, what if. . .?!?

So the very nature of the unconscious with our childhood survival strategies intact rejects our attempts at personal growth and development. Even learning a new skill can be threatening. We have developed a persona so we look "calm, cool, and collected" in the world. But nothing makes us look *less* cool than trying something new for the first time! Along with the fear of appearing ignorant, our unconscious reminds us that we've always been safe with our old way of doing things or with our old skill set. In trying something new, we might actually fail – and the unconscious is programmed not to fail! This is the origin of many of our false beliefs about ourselves. In creating our childhood survival strategies, we also created beliefs of what we are and are not capable of– which leads to limiting our growth.

Perception is Projection

We see what we expect to see, not what we don't expect to see. We see what is familiar to us, not what is totally out of our range of experience. The filters through which we perceive set us up to perceive people, places and things as safe/dangerous, good/bad, like me/not like me, pleasant/unpleasant. In general, for most of us, anything that smacks of real change is on the dangerous, bad, not like me, unpleasant side of the coin.

Cause & Effect

Even when we accept the necessity of change as demanded for personal growth, that change will not be as satisfying if we are not firmly at Cause in our lives. The person who is on the effect side of cause and effect will approach change as running *away* from something, rather than running *toward* something. The difference is not just in semantics. The energy of running *away* is avoidance and typically fear-based. Running away from a difficult or painful situation may appear to be personal growth, but it really is a move that "constricts" rather than expands your life. And when you run away from the dynamic of a situation without resolving it, typically you carry it with you.

For example, take the person who quits her job because she has an abusive boss. More often than not, she will find a similarly abusive boss or co-worker at her next job, and the next, and the next. Haven't you seen people who date the same "bad news" boyfriend or girlfriend over and over? New names but essentially the same person? It may appear that they are "growing" by getting out of a bad relationship. But the person who is at Effect is merely trying to avoid pain by moving away from it. There is no sense of empowerment in such a move, no real expansion or growth.

On the other hand, the person who has accepted himself or herself as Cause in her own life will approach change differently.

Rather than "I don't want this abusive situation," she will focus on the situation she *does* want. "I want to work in a company where there is mutual respect, appreciation, and collaboration where I can use my talents and skills to make a contribution." Can you sense how the outcome will be different? The person who is at Cause doesn't avoid pain but embraces expansion.

Creation / Dichotomies

In the process of change and personal growth, there is often a misunderstanding that is connected to the principle of creation and dichotomies. We may recognize that where we are or who we are is not where and who we want to be. Time for change. Good so far. But in our eagerness to implement change, often we go overboard running to the far end of the spectrum from where we began.

It's the classic mid-life crisis story: A guy wakes up one morning and looks at his life, which has become routine, boring, passionless. To compensate, he runs off with the secretary and buys himself a hot red sports car that he can't afford. Or maybe he wakes up and decides that his life has no purpose and his material trappings have no meaning. So he shaves his head and runs off to a monastery. The misunderstanding in both cases is that "if this is not good, its opposite must be."

Another common error is to embrace a teacher or system as "the only way." When you have experienced growth and insight from a particular teaching, it's natural to be enthusiastic. But the universe laughs whenever we plant our feet on the ground and exclaim, "This is it!" We are not meant to be planted but to be in constant movement. The opposite of "it" has been created at the exact same time to keep us moving. Our clinging to "one way" only slows down our natural expansion and makes it rougher on us.

The world is full of contrasts, and it does help to figure out what makes you feel alive and expansive – and what does not. But sustainable personal growth is not about leaping to extremes. Personal growth and development happens in increments. It's a journey meant to last your entire life, not a sprint to the finish.

Cycles & Rhythms

And within that journey, each of us has a particular rhythm. Some of us expand quickly and seemingly effortlessly. Others take their time to put the puzzle pieces together. The mistake people make is comparing the rhythm of their own personal growth to someone else's. How do you know that you're moving at a speed and rhythm that's right for you? Personally, I like to feel that I am being stretched but not stressed. I like to feel maybe slightly out of my depth, but not like I'm drowning. It's like a great exercise session: you feel that you're going a bit farther than you've gone before, but you're not injuring yourself in the process. If you feel like you're not even breaking a sweat, maybe it's time to pump it up.

Like every other area, personal growth and development happens in cycles. You may sometimes feel that you're coming around to the same old issue or place you were before, but you are actually in the same spot at a more subtle level. For example, you might have focused on becoming more responsive and less reactive in your relationship. Everything is going smoothly until one day – Wham!—you find that all of your buttons have been pushed and you feel like a crazed person! This doesn't necessarily mean that you've slipped backwards. Often, it simply means that you are peeling back another layer of the onion. It's not just déjà vu all over again. You have the opportunity to deepen your responsiveness this time around.

In all learning, there is a cycle that starts when you are completely ignorant. You then move to the stage where you have some knowledge but still no handle on the subject. Next, you feel like you have the basics then you begin to grasp the subtleties. Finally, you feel that you have enough knowledge that you can actually expand on that knowledge and add to it. And that's when, if you are keeping yourself on the cutting edge of growth and learning, you start feeling ignorant again. Misunderstanding the cycles within personal growth and development leads to frustration and discouragement. These cycles are natural – and necessary.

Conscious/Unconscious

Earlier in this chapter, we talked about the unconscious mind's resistance to change because it functions to make sure you survive – and change may threaten that survival. But that doesn't mean the unconscious is the enemy of growth. It's actually the powerhouse that can catapult your growth and development *if* you interact with it properly. The mistake we make is when we try to browbeat the unconscious mind into accepting the change that our conscious minds are determined to make. We bludgeon it with affirmations and try to bulldoze our way past its protests through sheer force of will. Sometimes this approach "works," but most of the time it merely sets up a bigger battle because using force causes the resistance to change to become stronger.

You can think of the unconscious as a five-year-old child who is good, sincere, always trying to help you and keep you safe from harm. When a five year old refuses to go into a room due to fear that demons and scary monsters reside there, you can certainly pick the screaming child up and throw him in anyway. But I think most of us would take a different approach. We would draw out the child's concerns and address them. Perhaps we would offer a "test run" by stepping just a few inches into the room at first. We might help the child become "armed" to face the demons. Most intelligent parents would find a way to coax the child into the room by allaying his fears and getting his cooperation.

This approach works better with the unconscious. On the path to personal growth with the many changes it requires, it's helpful to work with the unconscious and gain its cooperation. It is also important to remember that once a choice is made to change or work on something, following through and taking action are essential. Take the example of hiring a personal trainer to assist you with a workout. If you constantly call and say "Nope, not today. I'll see you tomorrow"– eventually that trainer will give up and not want to assist you. The same goes for your unconscious mind. Your unconscious mind wants to help but if you keep putting off action until a tomorrow that never comes, pretty soon your unconscious mind will give up, figuring that you aren't really serious about what you said you wanted.

Ecology

All of the areas of life fit together like puzzle pieces. Changes that you make toward personal growth will naturally affect all the other areas of your own life. But some of us neglect to notice how much our own personal growth affects the world around us: our families, community, country – even our planet. So the question still must be asked: Even though this change or personal expansion seems good for me, is it ultimately good for all beings and things in my sphere?

It's true that sometimes our personal growth is jarring for people around us. They are comfortable with who we have been and how we relate to them. As you move along your path and embrace your own expansion, others may feel threatened or uneasy. The question of "Is this good for them?" is not asking "Will everyone agree with my changes or feel totally comfortable with them?" They won't. But that doesn't mean you should give up on your own personal development. You may want to discuss your changes and why you are making them with people who are close to you. Many friends and family will support you. Others may not. Your relationship with them may be altered and you may even have to choose whether you can stay within that relationship at all.

But your relationships and being aware of the ecology within which you live can also be a motivation. In Buddhism, there is a practice called "establishing altruistic intention." It teaches that, as you seek to do anything, including becoming the best person you can be, you do it for the good of all humankind. The truth is that we are all inextricably connected. So your personal growth and development will add to the expansion and evolution of all of us.

Flexibility

Flexibility, the natural result of identifying and clearing childhood survival strategies and unconscious directives, is crucial in our personal growth. We simply don't know what we don't know. We don't know what's ahead because we are entering new territory, often without a map. Being in the midst of change, even if it's a change we desire, can feel unnerving. Often this is when our childhood survival strategies will rise up again to take control! We need to stay vigilant and be aware of when we are reacting rather than responding to the uncertainties inherent in personal growth.

In personal growth, there can be a misunderstanding that being "flexible" means losing yourself. The mistake here is thinking that "who we are" is based on how we have dealt with life in the past via our childhood survival strategies and persona. But that's a false identification. As we peel away the layers of the onion, who we really are is at the core. It is not our behaviors or reactions. The intention of personal growth is to get to that core and discover all the magic we possess when we clear away the self-imposed limitations. Personal growth does not change this core. It reveals it.

Where to Start

Flourishing in personal growth and development is an attitude of constant curiosity and openness. It's like being in a beautiful mansion with long hallways and many doors. You begin by following a thread of something that catches your attention. Maybe it's something that excites you – or maybe it's a part of your life that makes you crazy! In either case, follow that thread into whatever room it leads you. Explore that room, and when you feel complete, head back out into the hallway and follow another thread. Trust me, you'll never run out of rooms to explore! It's a life-long endeavor.

Chapter 8: Inner Technology

Some of you may not be familiar with the term "inner technology." Inner technology is comprised of those capacities and abilities that we each have inside us including such things as intuition, telekinesis, energy healing, telepathy, and clairvoyance. Though these skills lie dormant in most of us, prior to the advent of agriculture, humankind lived and survived by these abilities. As hunter-gatherers, we relied on these abilities to help us find food, avoid danger, and repair wounds. But as we developed more "external technology," we moved away from our innate inner technologies. People who continued to practice them were considered miracle workers, saints, or witches.

Today, we can seed clouds with chemicals to produce rain rather than pray for it. (By the way, the inner technology that produced rain has been called the "fifth mode." It was not a petition to receive rain in the future but a statement of the "truth" of rain in the present.) We use the internet rather than tapping the collective unconscious and we watch TV to know what the weather is doing. X-rays and blood tests diagnose us; drugs and surgeries heal us. We have scads of data at our disposal to make decisions and we communicate with each other via phone, email, and text. Our electric blankets keep us warm and our smoke detector alerts us of impending danger.

With all of our sophisticated external technology, why would we even bother with those inner technologies?

Empowerment

Without these inner technologies, we cannot be fully empowered. Our external technologies are clever, but incomplete. The full knowing that can be tapped in the collective unconscious has not only data and information but also a wisdom and perspective the internet does not have. Conventional healing through drugs and surgeries often creates imbalance in the body system, which in turn causes other health issues. When we communicate electronically, especially in abbreviated mediums such as texting, we are not communicating the full breadth, energy, and experience of the message.

By relying on external technologies solely, we are at their mercy. When conventional medicine cannot find a drug or treatment to attack a disease, it is pronounced incurable. If we can't get sufficient data or enough "consumer ratings" online, we might feel helpless about making a decision. If the power goes out, we feel helpless to stay warm and if our cell batteries die we have no way to get in touch with others!

We renounced our inner technology for external technologies and elevated our analytical thinking to become the "be all and end all." Everything must pass the tests and measures of our conscious, rational minds to be "valid" in today's world. But as

Albert Einstein said, "The intuitive mind is a sacred gift and the

rational mind is a faithful servant. We have created a society that

honors the servant and has forgotten the gift." If one of the

greatest thinkers of the twentieth century values this inner

technology, it just might be something worth studying.

(Fortunately, intuition is one of the inner technologies that is

gaining more acceptance in modern culture.) Most importantly,

opening to the powers of our inner technologies reminds us that

our "inner" realities are as valid as (or perhaps *more* valid than)

"external" realities.

Sympathetic vs. Para-sympathetic System

The key to accessing our inner technology lies in the

parasympathetic nervous system. This is the system that controls

relaxation, where your breathing is deep and slow, and you see

with the "soft eyes" of peripheral vision. It's the state that athletes might describe as The Zone, when all senses are alive,

focused, and completely calm. Others might call it "mindfulness"

as in attentiveness solely to the present moment without

wandering into the past or future. Within this state, we are able

to access our inner technologies.

In contrast, the sympathetic nervous system controls our ability to

react to danger as in the flight, fight, or freeze response. The

sympathetic nervous system releases adrenalin and cortisol to the

body and redirects blood flow to muscles and away from organs.

Our pupils dilate to let in more light and sharpen our vision. In this

state, our pulse races and breathing becomes faster to ready us to

face the emergency before us.

In centuries past, humans used their sympathetic nervous systems

about 5% of the time and spent the rest in the more relaxed

states of the parasympathetic system. But today, that ratio is

reversed. Most of us spend the vast majority of our days racing, struggling, battling, avoiding, trying to catch up. We are painfully aware of and controlled by our clocks and calendars. We can never do enough and we can never get it all done. To deal with the pressures of the contemporary life we've created, our sympathetic nervous system floods our bodies with cortisol and adrenalin almost constantly.

The only method we have to signal our parasympathetic nervous system to kick in is through our breathing and going into peripheral vision and grounding ourselves. We can't intentionally slow down our heart rate (though skilled yogis have claimed that they can do this) or constrict our pupils or pull blood flow back to our organs and brains. But we can take deep slow belly breaths, which will signal the unconscious that all is well and safe. In turn, the unconscious directs the parasympathetic system to kick in. Sounds simple, doesn't it? But how many of us consciously do this throughout our day?

Finding Balance

In Chapter Five, we talked about the physical repercussions of our over-active sympathetic systems. Another major effect is that being in this state constantly prevents us from accessing the inner technologies that are our inherent gifts. For most of us, the point is not to abandon modern life, quit our jobs, leave our families, and seek out a cave or an ashram for the rest of our days. Instead, our assignment is to balance the rush and hurry with the depth and slower pace of the parasympathetic system. We aren't meant to deny our analytical minds but to add the wisdom of our intuition into our decisions. Many of the inner technologies take time and concentration to cultivate. But in the beginning, it is enough to spend more time in the parasympathetic state that is calm, relaxed, and open.

Childhood Strategies and Inner Technology

I think many of us remember times as children when our inner technologies were more present. We had small moments of telepathy or intuition. But unless these gifts are acknowledged and nurtured – which is fairly rare in western culture – they quickly disappear. As small, vulnerable human beings, our first objective is survival, which is the realm of the sympathetic nervous system. The strategies we develop to survive are created while we are in survival mode and therefore have the characteristics of the sympathetic system. If a child chooses the passive/aggressive strategy, he has really opted for a "flight then fight" response. The child who tries to be "invisible" mimics the survival mechanism of many creatures (chameleons, turtles, dragon lizards) as does the one who tries to "fit in" to be safe.

So our childhood survival strategies are the product of our sympathetic nervous systems *and* these strategies ensure that we keep operating with the sympathetic nervous system in full force.

We stay busy protecting ourselves and resolving (or avoiding)

issues externally. If as adults we cling to these strategies, our

inner technologies cannot make themselves known. In this

survival mode, we have trouble identifying the strategies that

obstruct our growth. But when we consciously choose to relax

and breathe deeply, when we consciously choose to look inward

rather than outward, we have access to our inner technologies

and we have the ability to identify and dismantle the survival

strategies that no longer serve us.

Perception is Projection

If we don't understand perception is projection correctly, our

access to our inner technologies is impossible. People who believe

that the external world as they see it is an ultimate truth or reality

will have difficulty investigating and allowing the realities of the

inner world.

Once perception is projection is fully understood and embraced, this principle opens up many possibilities for expanding awareness in inner technology. For example, the Essenes (a mystical sect of Judaism that existed from about 2nd century BC to the 1st century AD) used the Seven Mirrors[4] as a tool for growth. The Essenes (one of whom is rumored to be Jesus of Nazareth) used each "mirror" for specific self-reflection. The first mirror reflects that which we are - our errors or wounds. The second shows us that which we judge or have an emotional charge about. The third mirror reflects back our losses and the fourth shows a forgotten love or cherished way of life. The fifth mirror reveals our connection to mother or father while the sixth displays our quest for the dark night of the soul or our challenge to growth. The seventh mirror reflects back our perception of ourselves, which determines how others will treat us. By using these internal mirrors, the Essenes recaptured the internal power that others had handed over to the external world.

---

[4] Gregg Braden - The 7 Essene Mirrors" on YouTube, May 6, 2012 (http://www.youtube.com/watch?v=EiBsczafvaA

Cause & Effect

When we place all of our belief in external reality and operate in
the survival mode of the sympathetic nervous system, we cannot
experience ourselves as Cause. When we're revved up with
adrenalin coursing through our veins, it's almost as if our fight or
flight reactions are in control and we have no choice in our
emotions. "That 'danger' out there has caused me to feel this
way!" But if we think that what happens in the external world
determines how we feel or think, we've placed ourselves on the
Effect (victim) side of the equation. Cause is not about
manipulating an external situation so you feel better internally.
It's about knowing that you have the ability to choose your
internal response no matter what the external situation.

We only truly experience ourselves at Cause when we calmly
focus on our inner realities and inner technology – and we can't
do that when our sympathetic nervous system is firing. Creating a

balance in our hectic lifestyles allows us a better connection to our inner technology. When we allow ourselves the time to slow down, to connect, and to listen to our bodies, we gain a better understanding of not only our physical bodies but also our mental, emotional, and spiritual bodies. This alignment gives us more access to and a fuller connection with our inner technology.

Creation and Dichotomies

Dichotomies are caused by thoughts in our internal world that create opposites in the external world. Usually, we do this unconsciously and unintentionally. For example, if the internal thought you carry is "Everyone must behave," odds are good that you'll start seeing a lot of misbehaving in the world! But we can learn to use the principle of creation and dichotomies consciously in our lives to create balance, like balancing our sympathetic and parasympathetic states. When we have a balanced and focused outlook on what we want out of life and what we desire from others in our life, we then have a laser focus to create what we want and attract the right people to share our journey. Our clear focus allows things to line up for us so our desires can manifest. The clearer you are on what you want to create, the easier the path will lay out for you.

Cycles and Rhythms

The sympathetic nervous system and parasympathetic nervous system, when functioning optimally, have a natural rhythm and cycle that allow us to flourish. I'd suggest that operating from the sympathetic system 5% of the time and spending the remaining time in the parasympathetic state is optimal. Contemporary life has disrupted this natural cycle and our nervous systems are stuck on over-drive. However, we do have the ability to bring ourselves back to the healthy cycles of generations past when we consciously choose to do so.

This may seem out of reach for many people. But being in the parasympathetic state with its access to our inner technologies is really the simple practice of slowing down and being present in the moment. Our rational minds may fear that we'll "get less done" and "fall behind" if we do this. But as many of us have experienced, we are actually more productive, creative, and effective when we are relaxed and tapping inner resources. We've also seen how much more smoothly our lives seem to unfold when we start and end our day with a period of silence, contemplation, or meditation.

Conscious Mind/ Unconscious Mind

We previously used the analogy of a vast cavern to describe the unconscious mind and a tiny penlight as the conscious mind. Our inner technologies are housed within this vast cavern, as are the controls that regulate our sympathetic and parasympathetic nervous systems. Even though the conscious mind may start the process by being interested in inner technology and by choosing to relax into an open state, it isn't really the conscious mind's job to learn inner technology. It's as if the conscious mind opens the door but then steps out of the way to allow the process of learning to unfold. If the conscious mind tries too hard to understand, prove, verify and "get it right," our inner technologies remain elusive.

This is where the saying "Let go and let flow" comes into play. I mentor a student who constantly challenges this concept. Instead of allowing her process to unfold, she overanalyzes each situation then wonders why she feels like she's beating her head against a wall. When she lets go of how the process is working, the answers she seeks will come to her easily. The less force you put on it, the more easily it will unfold. Not to say that it doesn't take some effort. It does. It's about nudging things along to get the wheels moving versus trying to pull the load by yourself. It's simple – but not necessarily easy!

Ecology

External technologies are not able to take all aspects of life into

consideration. They have a narrow focus that does not

incorporate the well-being of those outside of that focus. For

example, conventional medical treatments for one part of the

body system often result in side effects that harm other parts.

Chemicals intended to produce more crops often deplete valuable

minerals in the soil, making for more plants that are less healthy

for us. Cell phones that make constant communication easier

have also been shown to increase traffic accidents. The vast reach

of the internet has increased our access to data but it has also

decreased our privacy and the safety of our children. Well-

meaning as it is, external technology simply does not have the

capacity to consider its effects on the entire ecology.

Inner technology does. How often are we reminded that the inner

technology of intuition is more all-encompassing than the data we've collected? For example, our "gut feeling" or intuition warns us not to accept a job that seems to be perfect for us – only to discover that this "perfect job" comes with a monstrous boss or that a better job is right around the corner. The inner technology of energy healing not only has no negative side effects but it often also addresses emotional issues surrounding the physical issue.

Also, though inner technologies can be used to affect the external, external technologies won't affect the internal. The inner technologies can be used to affect the external world, because what you change within yourself will cause change in the outer world. What is important is to avoid letting the common reality in the external determine your sense of yourself or your choices. For example, Ho'oponopono is an internal practice from Huna. It is an in-depth forgiveness process that is done entirely inside your own mind. However, the effects of the practice are often felt by the person on whom the forgiveness is focused and the external relationship is transformed. Meditation has been shown to positively affect physical symptoms of chronic pain, fibromyalgia, cancers, and coronary heart disease.

As mankind has evolved over time and as we've gained more external technologies, we have lost many of our internal technologies – and we have lost the balance. The question is: Do you choose to be at Effect and let the external run you? Or do you choose to be at Cause and exchange your external criteria for an internal gauge? To truly flourish, it's important to trust your internal check and let go of the need to rely on the external for reinforcement.

Flexibility

When operating via the sympathetic nervous system, we have very little flexibility in our responses. The cortisol and adrenalin coursing through our bodies, especially if we've been highly stressed over long periods of time, make us more volatile, emotional and pumped up to defend ourselves. In this state, we're usually not able to weigh options or consider alternatives or be flexible at all. Our very bodies are telling us what we need to do to survive!

Moving into the relaxed parasympathetic state, we know we have more choices. We can be calm, rational, and objective, and decide how to respond rather than react. By slowing down further and accessing our inner technology, we realize that we have even more choices in our response. Our intuition offers deeper wisdom and insight. Our ability to sense energy helps us interact and communicate with others more effectively.

Chapter 9: History

I really can't overemphasize how important studying history is for a life to flourish. It's an incredible source of information and insight that is critical to our growth. As author/activist James Baldwin said, "People are trapped in history and history is trapped in them."

History includes not only your personal history but also the history of your family, your community, your country and culture, humanity, and the planet. All of this history has shaped who you are today and is the foundation of who you seek to be in the future. It's in your physical DNA and the way your brain is wired. It shows up in how you relate to your children and the air you breathe. History determines the political system under which you live and your concept of God. The conglomeration of history, from personal to planetary, brings you as who you are to this very moment in time.

Cycles and Rhythms

When you study history, you're essentially studying cycles and rhythms. These rhythms and cycles are reflected and repeated in the moments of the present, but it's hard to see them in the present. It's the forest for the trees syndrome. As former Secretary of Health, Education, and Welfare, John W. Gardner noted, "History never looks like history when you are living through it." As we face the situations and issues of each day, we get caught up in our own drama as if it is the only play in town and we are the only ones acting it out based on a script that has never been seen before.

We also miss seeing our own patterns because we do them "professionally" at the unconscious level. We are so skilled in them that we no longer think about them or even notice them.

We're like fish in water, not even noticing that we're wet because

it's so integral to how we've always been. Using the broad

perspective of history, these rhythms and cycles become more

obvious.

On a personal level, the value of history is that you can spot your

own patterns. From the time you were a child until today, how did

you approach the unknown? How did you deal with

disappointment? What did you do to feel worthy? You'll find that

you've repeated certain patterns for decades – and are probably

repeating them now. But once you are aware of your personal

patterns, you can choose to maintain or make changes as

appropriate. In other words, having a grasp of history is very

empowering!

History does repeat itself but not in its exact same form. It works

in the way that cycles work: you come back to the same place but

from a different vantage point. For example, World War II was not an exact replica of World War I, but it had some striking

similarities in the way it was fought, the issues at stake, and even

the characters in play. But they differed in many ways. World War

I was instigated to gain control by using force. The Second World

War was instigated by people who already had power but wanted

to keep it and expand their reach to the whole world. They both

used force but external force is not power. True power is internal.

When people try to change the common reality by using force, it

always blows up in their face because it is a false power.

Patterns do not necessarily replicate themselves exactly either.

You may not demean your wife's housekeeping abilities as your

father did, but you may show disrespect for her career

aspirations. Our country may not be as overtly prejudicial against

racial minorities as it was in the nineteenth century, but it

certainly has not become color blind and comfortably integrated.

The patterns might wear different clothes but unless you have identified them and consciously chosen to re-frame them, they

are still alive and kicking.

Childhood Survival Strategies and History

For many of us, the access point for identifying our childhood

survival strategies is through studying our personal history. Often,

by stepping back and viewing the past, we can clearly see the

defense mechanisms we chose to be safe. We can also view the

histories of family members to see these strategies. Families, as

we'll see in the next chapter, form an overall dynamic as a unit.

The players fit like an intricate puzzle, feeding each other and

feeding *off* one another. Often your own patterns are reflected in

other members of your family. For example, if your sister

exploded with blame and criticism when confronted with a

disappointment, is it possible you do the same? Or is it possible

that you learned to do the opposite in order to play your part in

the family dynamic?

A mistake people can make in reviewing their history and discovering childhood strategies is in staying stuck in the sense of guilt. For example, when I identified my own passive/aggressive survival strategy, I reviewed all of the situations in which I had used this strategy over the decades of my life. And I had to come to terms with the pain I had caused others. It was not a pleasant realization. But if I had stayed stuck in the shame and self-recrimination I felt at that time, I would not have improved my life and my relationships one whit. In a funny way, guilt can feel comforting—but it also keeps us from doing the work we need to do to make positive and lasting change in our lives.

Perception is Projection

Jessamyn West who wrote the famous novel, *The Friendly Persuasion,* once said, "The past is really almost as much a work of the imagination as the future." In other words, the history we see, especially of our personal lives, is more about our projections than what actually happened. Have you ever started reminiscing with a friend or family member about an incident in the past, only to realize that your memories of the incident are totally different? You remember how angry your father was but she remembers him as serious but kind. He remembers how he felt left out and you remember him as the life of the party. She remembers how terrifying the storm was and you think to yourself, "What storm?"

Many people are stunned (or very reluctant) to see that <u>what</u> we remember is not real. It's jarring to realize that the truths about what happened in the past that helped you determine how to live were not truth at all. As Mark Twain said, "It ain't what you don't know that will get you into trouble. It's what you know for sure that just ain't so." Just like our perceptions of the present, our "history" has little to do with an external reality and everything to do with what we project out into the world. But though it may be fiction, it's *our* fiction and that is its value.

An exercise I like is to sit down and write out your histories: your personal and family history as well as the history of your community and country. You can include other histories if you like, such as the history of religion or your industry – whatever seems relevant to you. Once you have these histories written, step back and review them. What are the central themes you noted in them? Did you focus on disappointment, betrayal, failure? Did you write about successes, heroes, and hope? The very tone you use when you write about your histories will give you good information about what you project onto the world.

Cause & Effect

Reviewing our histories is also invaluable for seeing the cause and effect principle of life. *This* happened – which led to *this* happening. I had that belief and my experience then proved it "valid." When you acknowledge yourself as Cause, you can look back and see how perfectly it all played out. If we view just the narrow slice of life that is the present, it's sometimes hard to see

Cause & Effect in action. But taking the big perspective of history,

how we created the situations and results we've produced

become much more obvious.

But if you aren't at Cause, history can be misused. Rather than a

tool for learning, it can become a justification for staying stuck.

For example, the person who looks back and sees that she had an

abusive upbringing may end up using that as justification for

staying stuck in anxiety or fear. She may even begin to label

herself as "an abused child" which further solidifies the identity.

Unfortunately, some forms of therapy almost encourage this use

of history. The patient is asked to find the "culprits" of their past:

"My father yelled at me and beat me" or "My mother was cold

and unloving." As a victim, you now have an acceptable reason

and excuse for staying within your childhood survival strategies

and destructive habits. But is that really what you want?

When you stay on the cause side of the equation, you can view your history and use it to expand your life rather than constrict it. As author Norman Cousins wrote, "History is a vast early warning system." When you are at Cause, you realize that the actions and reactions of the past do not have to be repeated. You can choose to do it differently and respond differently.

Creation / Dichotomies

The principle of creation and dichotomies says that whenever we have a thought or action its opposite is immediately created. By studying history, you can begin to see this principle in action. Prior to understanding the principles, we create these opposites unconsciously. But looking back with our new understanding, we can see *how* we have created *what* we created in the past, as well as how these creations impact our present. And we can choose to balance the opposites in our lives or create something entirely different for ourselves.

Your history shows you the patterns and dichotomies you have created. For many of us, our history is a blueprint of "what not to do next time." We have discussed in earlier chapters about the relationships we create. Are we repeating the cycle over and over again or are we looking at the history and creating something different? In health and fitness, those individuals who realize what has worked or not worked in the past have the freedom to choose a different tactic that is more effective. But those who don't learn from history buy yet another exercise machine that they won't use or become "yo-yo dieters."

As you look at your history and see the unconscious creation of dichotomies that you don't want in your life, you might view that unwanted dichotomy as a mistake. But actually, dichotomies appear to help you determine what you want in life. The more contrast in your life, the more polar opposites you experience, the better you can see what you want and don't want. Even though this activity was unconscious in the past, it has value if you learn

from it.

Cycles & Rhythms

We talked about history as the study of cycles and patterns. One

of the biggest benefits of this study is that when you view what is

happening in the world – the economy, our culture, the planet –

through the lens of history, it's easier to remain detached,

compassionate, and understanding. You can see that the current

"catastrophe" is yet another position in the overall cycle. This

doesn't mean that you remain frozen or passive about the crisis,

but that your actions can be made from a broader vantage point

without the knee-jerk reactions you might have otherwise.

For example, most retailers are aware of the "retail cycle." They

know that sales will peak during certain times – Christmas

holidays, Back to School days, etc. They also know that sales are typically slow in months like May and August, so they don't flip

out and close their doors when that happens. They merely plan

accordingly, ramping up or reducing staff and inventory to match

the anticipated cycle.

Conscious/Unconscious

Studying history is mainly the work of the conscious mind. But as

you proceed, the unconscious mind may have quite a bit to

contribute. All of us have memories, decisions and strategies that

we developed in the past then stuffed into our unconscious – that

vast dark cavern. As you consciously review various aspects of

your histories, allow your unconscious to offer up threads to

follow and investigate. We do this by entering the

parasympathetic state, focusing on breathing, relaxing our minds

and paying attention to what pops up. As you delve into the study

of your history, you may also find that your dream life becomes

more vivid. This is another way the unconscious communicates.

Ecology

Unfortunately, often when we look at our histories from the point of view of ecology, we get to see the problems we create by not taking ecology into consideration in our decisions or actions. If we consider only the good of ourselves or a specific group of people, our accomplishments often disrupt the well-being of others. This is true across the board, from our personal histories to the history of our world. Whenever we attack a problem without encompassing the whole, we're bound to create other problems. This lesson is painfully clear as we review history. If nothing else, it might inspire us to more ecological thinking!

Hopefully, our study will also unearth examples of decisions or actions that were made from an ecological viewpoint. Life has existed on the planet for around 6 billion years. Natural life has evolved solutions over that time on the best way to do things. In contrast, our industrial society was created from a totally different perspective. Nature takes care of the waste and recycles it. Human industry creates then just discards the waste. As the industrial process continues to create more waste, nature has to find a way to balance it out (i.e. through storms and volcanoes). Many think there is not consciousness involved in Nature, but everything has consciousness. So you have ecology and ecology requires recycling. Our industrial society creates waste and tries to get rid of it – that's un-ecological! Nature works and supports life but human industry doesn't work and kills life. And now we are paying the price for that way of being.

Flexibility

The power in studying our histories lies in our ability to learn from them, re-frame them, and create more expansive, positive approaches to our lives. This is the epitome of flexibility. But first it's important to look back and discover where we were not flexible, where we were run by our childhood survival patterns and reacted in ways that did not serve us. It's those times when we felt "trapped," that we had no other option but to defend ourselves in a particular way.

Entertaining how we might have done something differently in the past is often easier to see (and less threatening!) than seeing how we might respond differently in present situations. And by using our history in this way, we set ourselves up to give ourselves options in the present.

Looking back on situations in your past, what if you had chosen a different response or perspective? How would that different choice potentially create a different present and future? This exercise shouldn't be used to beat yourself up! We all do the best we can with what we know and who we are at the time. So use this exercise to expand your future, not to create regrets for yourself.

Chapter 10: Family

Let's first take a look at the totally perfect family: Mom and Dad are fully conscious and awake, realizing that their job is to allow each child to blossom according to the intrinsic skills and preferences with which they were born. Being fully versed in the stages of childhood development, they would encourage each child's independence and experimentation with life as appropriate for each child's age. Children would experience themselves as fully nurtured, respected, and safe, absorbing only the most positive behaviors and responses to life's challenges.

Know many families like this? Me neither.

But good, bad, or indifferent, the family unit is the first physical environment most of us encounter. As vulnerable children, our nuclear and extended family is where our inherent personality type begins to emerge (to be accepted or not) and our innate gifts and predilections surface (to be encouraged or not). Our families provide the first examples of the basic principles of life, such as creation and dichotomies, perception is projection and cause and effect. The family unit is the ecosystem within which we learn to protect ourselves by developing our childhood survival strategies.

Basic Personality Types

Many cultures view children as "blank slates" who must be formed and shaped by their families, notably their parents. But we all enter this world with our own unique personality type. Early in the twentieth century, Carl Jung, the Swiss psychiatrist who founded analytical psychology, theorized that there are four principal psychological functions by which we experience the world. These functions are paired in three dichotomies representing how we "judge" the rational world (thinking versus feeling) and how we "perceive" the irrational world (sensing

198

versus intuition). Based on this theory, Katharine Cook Briggs and her daughter, Isabel Briggs Meyers, developed a questionnaire to determine an individual's psychological preferences to ascertain his or her personality type. Over time, they and others added more dichotomies: the dichotomy of attitude (extroverted versus introverted) and how a person dominantly relates to the outside world (judging versus perceiving).

The Meyers-Briggs Test assesses which side of each dichotomy is dominant in an individual. Sixteen combinations of these dichotomies are possible, creating the possibility of sixteen different personality "types." For example, according to contemporary Meyers-Briggs users, an INTJ (introvert, intuitive, thinker, judger) will have a tendency to be skeptical and independent, and an original thinker with great drive for achieving his goals. An ESFP (extrovert, senser, feeler, perceiver) will tend to be spontaneous with an exuberant love of life and fun. Neither side of any dichotomy is right or wrong, and no personality type is better or worse than another.

Personality Differences in the Family

Our personality types determine in part how we process the world, and most human beings assume – incorrectly – that others are processing the world exactly as they process it. Sometimes, parents and children have same or similar personality types, which makes the relationship run more smoothly – at least until the natural rebellion of puberty kicks in! People with the same type naturally understand each other's desires and motivations. They know how to communicate and interact with one another to be understood and accepted. They approach problem solving and express emotions similarly. Basically, they speak the same language.

But in looking at the members of most families, it's almost like a session of the United Nations where everyone speaks a different language and needs a translator! It's pretty clear that children are often different types than their parents. Some parents respect this and do their best to translate into their children's language. But parents who are unaware of how different types operate or who subscribe to the "blank slate" theory, often wrongly assume that their child is (or should be) their same personality type and that child does (or should) process the world as they do and does (or should) speak the same language. This doesn't work out well because personality is inherent. Assuming that a child with a different personality type can process things exactly as the parent processes them or trying to get a child to be who he is not causes frustration in the parent and confusion (and sometimes damage) in the child.

Talents, Gifts and Interests

Along with our personality type, we also enter life with our own unique set of talents and interests. Even as babies and toddlers before they have had much exposure to the world, children can show a strong connection to music or to building things or to nature. They might be fascinated and good at sports or love to read and learn. Some parents recognize and nurture these unique gifts and interests in their children. Sadly, other parents are blind to their child's gifts and interests – or they do not value them. If a budding classical violinist born into a family of jocks is not valued, her self-esteem will take a big hit as she struggles to find her place in the family, as will the young athlete who is not valued in a family of artists.

Childhood Survival Strategies

We have talked about survival strategies children develop to protect themselves from their parents whether the threat is to their physical or emotional well-being. Young children are completely dependent on their parents for food, shelter, and emotional support. The family is the child's first environment, the first place where she needs to figure out how to survive and get those things she needs. So she may become passive and compliant to avoid her father's ire or rebellious to counteract her mother's smothering. He may choose to be passive/aggressive to avoid his mother's condemnation or shut himself off emotionally to cope with his father's lack of attention.

One of the most basic survival instincts is to "fit in" with the tribe or family unit to find protection from threats outside. To do this, a child develops survival strategies to keep himself safely within the unit. For example, a child who is an ENTP (extrovert, intuitive, thinker, perceiver) is quick and ingenious and bored by routine. But if his father is an ESTJ (extrovert, sensor, thinker, judger), Dad approaches the world differently. He will be more practical, organized, and attentive to detail. Can you see how the two might clash? Unless the father values the way his son processes life, he'll most likely see the child as flakey and unreliable. A child will somehow find a strategy to stay within the pack. He might keep silent about his unconventional ideas, pretend not to be as bright as he is, or struggle to be more organized in a way his father can appreciate.

And what about the child whose gifts and interests aren't appreciated by her parents? If she doesn't share the intrinsic talents of the rest of the family, she will likely feel that something is wrong or lacking in herself. Odds are that she will deny her own gifts or interests to fit in, and by the time she's an adult, she may have forgotten about them completely. To survive, she may even try to follow in her parents' footsteps, only to feel dissatisfied and lost as an adult.

Perception is Projection

We enter life, not as a blank slate, but with various qualities, characteristics, and preferences for dealing with the world. These intrinsic characteristics with which we are born mean that we enter life with some filters already in place. Aspects of our personality that are part of us are our gifts and our strengths. At birth, we have complete understanding of everything. But as we grow, the external environment with its beliefs and messages begins to overwhelm our internal knowing. In response, we create beliefs and the strategies that limit us. A child is not born as a blank slate. Each of us is born with everything we need. As we grow, we then accumulate a lot of not-so-helpful "stuff" that can be many generations in the making.

We also create the filters through which we see life from our culture and our religion, but we mainly take our cues from our families – especially our parents. Some of these filters are taught consciously. "All politicians are dishonest." "Criminals are sinners and can never be rehabilitated." "Work isn't supposed to be fun. That's why they call it work."

But many of the filters are taught by our parents unconsciously through their attitudes and behaviors. If your mother rolls her eyes whenever her husband expresses an opinion or your father turns away from beggars on the street, they are unconsciously teaching you who does not deserve respect. When they live in fear of taking risks or hoard money, they are showing you what you can expect out of life.

Cause & Effect

You begin to learn about cause and effect from infancy. You lie in your crib screaming and someone comes to pick you up. You spit up your milk and your mother frowns. Very early on, we recognize that what we do causes something to happen. But generally

206

before the age of seven, as little children who are totally dependent upon our parents for our survival, we don't feel very powerful. We eat and sleep on their schedule. We can explore only those environments they want us to explore and interact only with people they choose. We are told what to do and when to do it.

Some parents even attempt to maintain this level of control even after their children are grown. They continue to direct and manipulate their adult children's activities. But parents who want to see their children flourish in life help even their young children to become independent in age-appropriate ways. They allow them to choose new foods to try or what clothes to wear. They teach them skills like tying shoes or riding bikes. And most importantly, they allow their children to make mistakes and feel the natural consequences, to fall down and figure out how to get back up. As many of us would agree, it's the mistakes or failures in life that teach us the most – not the successes.

Parents also teach the basic principle of cause and effect by their own relationship to it. If parents see themselves as victims of what life hands them, it's almost inevitable that their children will absorb this stance as truth. On the other hand, parents who acknowledge responsibility for what happens in their lives provide a very empowered model for children to follow.

Creation / Dichotomies

Dichotomies are really the contrasts in life and contrasts allow us to figure out what we want and what we don't want, who we are and who we aren't. The family unit provides our first involvement with contrasts. And just as mistakes are our best teachers, so are contrasts. The experience of similarities doesn't really help us define what we want and who we are – but when we run into contrasts, it becomes clear.

For example, if a child is a loving, caring nurturer who grows up in a household of loving, caring nurturers, he may not really recognize who he is. He may assume that those characteristics are universal. But if this loving, caring nurturer grows up in a household of uncaring manipulators, he will recognize that difference. He may not understand it fully or know what to do about it. He may feel inadequate because he is not "like" the rest of the family. But the contrast does force him to acknowledge who he is to some extent because of the contrast to the rest of the family unit.

Contrast within the family is the beginning of a natural process of self-definition. However, if parents are not willing to allow or respect contrast, that self-definition becomes more difficult and confusing. For example, if an ambitious child who wants a higher education is born to a family of factory workers, she may be told that she is "too full of herself," "pushy," or that she is "reaching beyond her station." She may have trouble identifying herself as bright and motivated. If down the road she does acknowledge who she really is and she is successful at tapping her potential, she might even be painted as "the black sheep" of the family because she did not conform!

Cycles & Rhythms

Each individual operates with four aspects (physical, emotional, mental, and spiritual) and each aspect has its own cycle and rhythm. More often than not, these aspects are on different parts of the cycle at any point in time. Your mental faculty may be waning while your physical cycle is waxing. Part of our journey is to figure out how our own aspects cycle, how to relate to the way they cycle and how to coordinate them.

When you are in a family unit, there are as many cycles and rhythms going on as there are people – times four! The odds of all cycles being in synch at any point in time are miniscule. The objective then is to figure out how to blend our own cycles with

others in the family and their cycles. The lessons we learn about

blending within the family unit can then be taken out into the

world where we find ourselves having to blend with everyone we

encounter and their cycles and rhythms – along with the cycles of

the country, the economy, nature, our planet, and the myriad of

other cycles surrounding us.

Again, this learning is a natural process. But many parents are not

aware of cycles and rhythms, which in turn will confuse their

children. Young children have an innate sense of their own cycles

and rhythms. They know when they need to rest, to eat, to

retreat, to engage. They know when they feel like being active

and when they want to do nothing. But if parents don't honor

these inherent cycles and rhythms, a child will struggle. Today's

parents seem driven to create jam-packed schedules for their

children, forcing these children to learn and engage in life at a pace that causes extreme stress and alienates them from their own natural cycles and rhythms.

Conscious/Unconscious

In the early years, children learn and absorb the world around them unconsciously. Before age seven, they are just beginning to define themselves and make conscious decisions or judgments. But their unconscious minds are fully active and engaged, identifying "dangers" and constantly devising survival strategies to ensure "safety." In a sense, parents (as all adults) who are not aware and awake are still operating as young children. They remain at the mercy of unconscious strategies that a 5 year old created.

Conscious parents, who have explored themselves and learned to express who they really are, are certainly better mentors for their children. Their main job is to help the child differentiate conscious responses from unconscious reactions. These parents allow their children to fall and get back up. They allow their children to learn the lessons "the hard way" which is actually Nature's way. Today, far too many parents protect their children from making the same mistakes they did growing up. This is a disservice to the children. In order to grow and flourish especially at a young age, we must allow our children to make mistakes, honor those mistakes, and learn from those mistakes. Our job as parents is to be there to help them walk through whatever they have created, rather than sheltering them from the learning they need to acquire through experience.

Ecology

The principle of ecology asks, "Is this decision good for me, my family, my community, my country, the planet?" As children begin to make conscious choices, they are typically only aware of the first part of the question: "Is this good for me?" As they begin to get a handle on that and choose according to what is good for themselves, they next bump up against the next part of the question: "Is this good for my family?" If children are fully integrated members of the family unit, this question will appear earlier rather than later.

But many parents do not fully integrate their children into the family ecology. By that, I mean, they do not take the child's unique needs into account when making decisions. For example, a father, in his efforts to be a good provider, may become a workaholic with no time or energy to give to his children at the end of the day. His decision to earn enough money to create a particular lifestyle for the family as a whole may be well intended, but it does not incorporate the emotional needs of his individual children.

Parents may also not fully integrate their children, by not showing them how each child's choices impact the whole. For example,

I've seen parents sacrifice their life savings to send a child to college. They don't want to "worry" the child so they don't let him know how this will impact their financial future. Again, though well intended, this disempowers a child. But parents who engage their children in this type of decision empower them. Working as partners, the parents and child could make choices about college and how to finance it in ways that are good for both of them.

Flexibility

Flexibility is having the ability to respond consciously rather than react unconsciously. The degree of flexibility we experience as adults is in direct proportion to how well we have identified and dismantled our unconscious childhood survival strategies. The point of the journey is to become who we really are and express that fully in the world. Our ability to be flexible in each area of life tells us how close we are to that goal.

Parents who are unaware react to life and their children rather than respond. Because parents are the ultimate authority figures, children (who do not yet have a grasp of conscious choices themselves) assume that these reactions are valid responses to whatever is going on. They in turn react unconsciously to their parents' reactions via their evolving survival strategies. It's a Catch-22 that does not support the child's flourishing.

When parents area able to openly express flexibility, and when they respond consciously rather than react unconsciously, children are quick to mimic this approach as soon as they are old enough to do so.

Family as the Classroom

Many spiritual teachers believe that we choose our parents and families, as well as the lessons we intend to learn, before we come into this existence. As such, the families to which we are born are the perfect settings for us. Functional or dysfunctional,

awake or asleep, happy and harmonious or full of painful conflict,

our time within the family unit as children provides a myriad of

opportunities to learn and grow, to define who we really are.

Many of us form the "issues" during our childhoods and don't get

to the resolutions of these issues. We carry a lot of

misunderstandings and baggage from those years, probably

because our parents had been carrying their own baggage. Our

job is to consciously re-frame that baggage, to re-create our

persona (that self that we present to the world) to more closely

align with who we really are.

The good news is that life offers us plenty of other opportunities

for growth and self-awareness. The bad news is that the more we

resist these lessons, the more painful they may become. Those

cosmic two by fours are not fun! They only appear to provide the

learning we requested.

About the Author

Samuel P. "Pat" Black III is founder of The Flourish Summit, communities designed to empower unconventional thinkers to flourish in the conventional world. Sparked by the challenges he experienced as a creative thinker, Black uses his knowledge, intuition, and creative gifts to inspire entrepreneurs, artists, researchers and other unconventional thinkers.

Black founded Erie Management Group, LLC (EMG) in 2004 to invest, create, and manage companies with innovative products capitalizing on economic opportunities in the Lake Erie Region. His groundbreaking companies include HERO Bx, LLC, one of the largest biodiesel manufacturers in the Northeast. He is also founder and president of the Blackstone Ranch Institute in Taos, New Mexico, which provides targeted seed money for innovative efforts in environmental sustainability, global carbon offset markets, sustainable business practices, renewable energies and green employment. Black and his wife, Susan, purchased 191 acres of pristine grassland in the Taos Valley to develop and demonstrate the best environmental practices for sustainable ranching and farming utilizing modern solar, wind, and geothermal technologies.

Black is co-founder and president of The Black Family Foundation, an active grant-maker, partner in philanthropy, catalyst, key convener, and leader in helping build vital, prosperous and sustainable enterprises. Since 1994, the Foundation has promoted innovation in education, health care, workforce development and the arts in the Erie region. The Foundation's philanthropic ventures work to spread knowledge, innovation, and environmentally sustainable practices in the United States and the developing world.

Black created The Flourish Summit communities to inspire

unconventional creative thinkers and spark innovations that

change the world. His initiatives exemplify his commitment to

create a new paradigm for unorthodox thinkers to thrive, create

and fulfill their genius. Learn more at www.FlourishSummit.com.

www.ingramcontent.com/pod-product-compliance
Lightning Source LLC
LaVergne TN
LVHW051504080426
835509LV00017B/1905